D1614399

MODERN ALGERIA

CHARLES-ROBERT
AGERON

Modern Algeria

*A History from 1830
to the Present*

TRANSLATED FROM THE FRENCH
AND EDITED BY
MICHAEL BRETT

HURST & COMPANY, LONDON

First published in French in 1964 by
Presses Universitaires de France
as *Histoire de l'Algérie contemporaine*
(9th edition 1990)

First published in English by
C. Hurst & Co. (Publishers) Ltd.,
38 King Street, London WC2E 8JT, England
Translation © C. Hurst & Co. (Publishers) Ltd., 1991
Printed in Hong Kong

ISBNs
Cased: 1 85065 027 6
Paper: 1 85065 106 X

PREFACE TO THE ENGLISH EDITION

The history of modern Algeria is nothing if not impassioned, in the making and the telling. The emotions aroused by the French conquest in 1830 have continued to the present day, always strong and often fierce. Their strength and their ferocity generated a civil war of murderous intensity and no very happy end, whose outcome left the fundamental issue of the country's development unresolved, economically, politically, and especially culturally. Quite apart from the basic problems of privilege and poverty, the questions of national character and personal identity which were raised by the opposition between colonisers and colonised during 132 years of French rule survived to govern the policies and outlook of hard-won independence. These questions were questions of history, to which French and Muslims both appealed for justification of their cause. While the fight for Algeria's future resumed with fresh force and occasional violence in the years following the departure of the French in 1962, the struggle for the country's past continued unabated as the colonial dispute over rights and wrongs passed into argument over success and failure in the long battle between natives and immigrants since the Carthaginians arrived in North Africa. The irony of the controversy is expressed in Jacques Berque's verdict, that by the time the conflict of colonisers and colonised came to a head, each side was ✓ fighting for what it was not, or was no longer; in other words, that modern nationalists were fighting in the name of a traditional society and culture irretrievably altered by foreign rule, while the Europeans who clung to power had effectively relinquished their grip upon the land they had originally colonised and still claimed to own.[1] Nevertheless, the argument has effectively determined our way of looking at Algeria since 1800, not to speak of the more distant past. It is a history that is not merely passionate, but lively in the extreme.

From the outside, it is a subject that may well seem self-centred and enclosed, imploding in internal strife. Certainly

[1] Jacques Berque, *Le Maghreb entre deux guerres* Paris, 1962 and 1969, 459; Eng. trans., *French North Africa*, London, 1967, 390.

⌐it is true that by incorporating Algeria into France, while at
the same time keeping it as far as possible separate from the
metropolitan country, the French isolated its affairs from the
world, and for a hundred years rendered its problems paro-
⌐chial. Fundamental issues were ruled by the technicalities of
French local government and administration. Meanwhile as
a tourist resort, reassuringly French and excitingly Islamic,
Algeria generated a travel literature in which it appeared,
literally and metaphorically, as an oasis, exotically picturesque.
Yet when its problems did finally come to a head, the result
was an explosion which resounded far beyond the borders of
Algeria, or even France. 'These prodigious peripeties', as Elie
Kedourie called them,[2] which included the overthrow of the
Fourth French Republic in 1958, extended through the coming
of de Gaulle as President of the Fifth Republic to the restructuring of NATO and the independence of French Black Africa,
while French participation in the Suez expedition of 1956, in
retaliation for Egyptian aid to the Algerian rebels, precipitated
the collapse of the old imperial order in the Middle East. Algeria
itself emerged with immense prestige as an example to be
followed by a Third World in search of revolutionary change.
Its history became, not only passionate and lively, but a matter
of concern to the world at large.

Charles-Robert Ageron first offered that history for our
inspection in 1964, two years after Algerian independence. His
Histoire de l'Algérie contemporaine, published for a wide audience
in the PUF *Que sais-je?* series, was not only a balanced and
scholarly account of its subject, but a firm contribution to the
controversy inseparable from the subject-matter. In measured
terms, and measured tones, it put the blame for the Algerian
war firmly on the European population of the country. Such
a view was inevitably attacked by those who held that France
itself was the culprit, who blamed the Muslim enemy, or conversely regarded the war of liberation as the necessary triumph
of the Muslim people. Even now, in the latest study to be published in English, he is accused of failure to comprehend 'the

[2] E. Kedourie, 'The retreat from Algeria', in idem, *Islam in the Modern World*,
London, 1980.

role of the settlers'.[3] The judgement, however, still stands, buttressed over the years by the author's immense scholarly output. Supported in this way, the *Histoire* of 1964 has become a classic statement of its case, and a classic in its own right, a masterpiece of historical writing never emulated, let alone surpassed in its field. Nor is it in any way a fossil, embedded in the strata of a bygone age. In the course of its nine editions, 1964–90, it has been extended by the author to cover, with necessary brevity, the experience of the years since Ben Bella first established himself as President of the new Republic. For this, the English edition, he has added the account of the last two dramatic years, since the riots of October 1988 precipitated the introduction of multi-party politics and the prospect of a wholly new regime. His verdict upon the history of independent Algeria is necessarily restrained; the time for conclusions of the kind that were possible on the colonial period in 1964 is not yet come. The reader will nevertheless detect the same liberal sympathies for people in search of liberty, equality and fraternity which govern his description of French rule, and infer the criticism that the one-party state which was established in 1962 was an unnecessary product of the Algerian revolution.

Described in this way, *A History of Modern Algeria* may well seem circumscribed by its own very special subject, the author a protagonist in an exclusive debate. Charles-Robert Ageron, on the contrary, has not only concerned himself with the wider effects of Algeria upon France. Increasingly, he has turned to the question of France in relation to the French empire as a whole, and especially to the subject of decolonisation. Indeed, as President of the Société Française d'Histoire d'Outre-Mer, with its major journal the *Revue Française d'Histoire d'Outre-Mer*, he may be said to be responsible, in no small measure, for the study of these matters in France today. His own publications, including his most recent *Histoire de la France coloniale*, of which the second volume, on decolonisation, has already appeared, fully reflect this interest, and set his work on Algeria firmly in a broader context. *A History of Modern Algeria* stands as an

---

[3] David Prochaska, *Making Algeria French*, Cambridge and Paris, 1990, 5 and 261, nn. 18–20.

indispensable contribution to the understanding of Algeria's crucial role in the history of the nineteenth and twentieth centuries, and anticipates what may yet prove an equally influential future.

The English edition has been prepared on the basis of the ninth French edition, 1990, with a fresh conclusion by the author. By comparison with the French edition, the English text has been lightly expanded for the benefit of readers who may not have sufficient knowledge of either French history or Algeria itself to be familiar with the political and geographical background. Where the narrative itself has been slightly extended to provide further information and explanation of events, this has been done as far as possible with reference to the author's other works. The bibliography is designed to serve the purpose of the translation, namely to introduce the work to the English-language reader as a starting-point of the inquiry into Algeria's place in history.

Grateful acknowledgement is due to Sebastian Ballard of the Department of Geography, School of Oriental and African Studies, who originated the four maps.

School of Oriental and African Studies,   MICHAEL BRETT
London,
February 1991

CONTENTS

MAPS

1
INTRODUCTION: ALGERIA BEFORE 1830 AND THE ALGIERS EXPEDITION

Should we begin the history of modern Algeria, as usual, in 1830? The name 'Algeria' certainly dates from 1831, but the Regency of Algiers, founded by the corsairs 'Arūj and Khayr al-Dīn and ruled by the Turks until the French conquest, dates from the first half of the sixteenth century. Before that, the history of the central and the eastern Maghrib, *al-Maghrib al-awsaṭ* and *Ifrīqiya*, goes back a thousand years. By way of an introduction to the modern period, some reference to these long 'dark ages' of Arabs, Berbers and Turks is certainly desirable. Imperfectly known as they are, they have their moments of brilliance which might expect to be mentioned at this point.

To try to sum up this history in a few lines, however, would serve no real purpose. It is better to warn the reader in the words of one of the great French scholars of North Africa, the sociologist Robert Montagne, that 'this confused history hardly satisfies our legitimate desire to understand the mystery of Islamic civilisation in Africa by reading a few well-chosen pages'. I have therefore decided against an account of the rapid conquest of the country by the Arabs from the east in the seventh and eighth centuries, and the subsequent grandeur and decline of the native Berber states and kingdoms. Only the invasion of the Hilali Arabs in the eleventh century calls for special mention, since by introducing Arab nomads as distinct from Arab armies into a sparsely-populated North Africa, it permanently altered the structure of its society.[1] Over and above the clash of tribes, the essential feature of this early history of the central Maghrib is the decisive influence of Islam, rooted in the affections of the population by the Sufi brotherhoods or *ṭuruq* (sing. *ṭarīqa*), the marabouts (*mrabtin*, *murābiṭūn*) or holy

---

[1] On this controversial question, cf. e.g. M. Brett, 'Ibn Khaldun and the Arabisation of North Africa', *The Maghreb Review*, IV, 1 (1979), 9–16.

men, and the *shurafā'* (sing. *sharīf*), descendants of the Prophet.[2] It was these brotherhoods and lineages which, as they spread among the tribes to which they gave their names, progressively Islamised and gradually Arabised the lands of the Berbers, the autochthonous population whose languages survive in the more mountainous regions of North Africa. Together they gave its strongly oriental character to Algeria, a country long dedicated socially and culturally to its religion.

The Regency of Algiers

In the forefront for our purposes, the political disintegration of the Maghrib in the later Middle Ages led, from the sixteenth century onwards, to the domination of the region as far west as Morocco by the Ottoman Turks. These semi-Europeans brought to Africa the idea of frontiers and territorial sovereignty; they gave Algeria its basic shape, stretching from the Trara in the west to La Calle in the east, and from Algiers on the coast to Biskra and Ouargla on the edge of the desert to the south. But the Turks of this Ottoman regency, distant vassals of the Sultan at Istanbul, scarcely dreamed of making their mark on the country. Interested chiefly in the profits of Mediterranean piracy, this oligarchy of *rais* or corsairs[3] and janissaries or musketeers, composed, according to the malicious Haedo,[4] of 'Turks by birth and Turks by profession', long remained on the fringe of tribal society. The administration of the country was reduced to the profitable exploitation of the native population, which was treated like a Christian *ra'iyya* (pl. *ra'āyā*), a 'flock' of subjects liable to the payment of *kharāj* or tax.[5] Despite the incessant revolts of the Arab-Berber tribes, this colonial regime was in firm control of the coun-

[2] In French, *chorfa*.
[3] The *taïfa al-raïs* or *ṭā'ifa al-riyyās* was the corporation of sea-captains which was a major component of the Turkish regime.
[4] A Spanish ecclesiastic writing at the beginning of the seventeenth century.
[5] Not necessarily Christian; Islamic governments down to the Ottoman empire habitually distinguished between the *khāṣṣa* or ruling élite of warriors, secretaries and men of religion, and the *'amma* or common people, frequently called 'the flock'.

try, relying on privileged *makhzan* or militarised government tribes,[6] playing on the divisions and rivalries of the *çoffs* (tribal factions[7]) and utilising the influence of the *turuq* (Sufi brotherhoods) and their *zäwiyas* (lodges).[8]

At the beginning of the nineteenth century, the *deys* (rulers) were chosen by the *odjaq* (corps of janissaries),[9] and received from Istanbul a caftan of investiture. But although they corresponded regularly with the Grand Vizier, they ruled as absolute monarchs, assisted by a *diwan* (council) of five high Turkish officials. The regency was divided into four provinces: the region of Algiers or *dar al-Sultan*, so-called because it came under the direct rule of the *dey*, and the three *beyliks*, that of the East or province of Constantine; that of the West or province of Oran; and the province of Titteri in the centre, with its capital at Medea. Each was ruled by a *bey* assisted by a *khalifa* or lieutenant, who conveyed the taxes of the province to Algiers on appointed dates. In theory, these *beyliks* were divided into *outhans* (Ar. *watan*, pl. *awtān*), tribal 'homelands' under *qā'id*-s (commanders) of Turkish or native origin. But whole districts were practically independent, controlled only by *zmalas* or *smalas*, roving companies in their tented camps, or by a few garrisons.

The towns administered themselves. The various municipal offices, including the headships of the craft guilds and of the *berranis* (Ar. *barrāniyya*), the strangers to the city, belonged to titular holders who leased them to their agents. The small number of city-dwellers, known as the *hadriyya* or *baladiyya* and comprising perhaps five per cent of the total population, were

---

[6] *Makhzan*, lit. 'treasury' (origin of English 'magazine'), is the common North African expression for the pre-colonial state. It speaks volumes for an institution that was thus conceived primarily in fiscal terms.
[7] Arabic *saff*, pl. *sufūf*, traditional alliances dividing each tribe and each group of tribes.
[8] The *zäwiya* might vary from a house of prayer in the city to a vast monastic establishment in the countryside, commanding great wealth and large clienteles. The Arabic pl., frequently encountered for the Sufis themselves as well as their houses, is *zawāyā*, colloquially *zwaya*.
[9] *Odjaq* in Turkish means 'hearth', and specifically meant the small companies who shared the same cooking-pot and formed the basic units of the corps (424 at Algiers in 1830), each under an *oda-bashi* or 'head of the barrack-room'. The officers had the title of *buluk-bashi* (or 'company commander').

cut off from the rural masses, the *badāwī* or bedouin. Seeing themselves as almost of a different race, they were loathed in their turn by the *qabā'il* or tribes. The Europeans called them Moors because, in the coastal cities in particular, the dominant bourgeoisie was of Andalusian origin, as was a part of the small Jewish community. Both Moors and native Jews, who were despised by the believers, were generally artisans and small traders. External trade was almost entirely in the hands of more recent Italian Jewish immigrants from Livorno (Engl. Leghorn), the port of Florence, who had become sole bankers to the *deys*, and almost 'kings of Algiers' as a result of the decline of piracy and the consequent financial crisis of the state. The total population of the country in 1830 is not known, since the Turks never carried out a census. Contemporary Muslim estimates varied from 2,250,000 (Abu Darba) to 10 million (Sidi Hamdan). From later statistics, the most reasonable estimate would seem to be 3 million, the figure given in the report of the intelligence officer Boutin in 1808, and in the correspondence of the French consul Dubois-Thainville who assisted him.

On the eve of the French expedition, the Turkish regime had become greatly weakened by various factors. These included widespread revolts led by the Darqāwa brotherhood, the growing independence of its officials, and the drop in exports. Even though several Kouloughli[10] families had successfully merged into the Turkish oligarchy, and various nobles of the Constantinois, the eastern province, had married into the families of the *beys*, anti-Turkish feeling remained strong among the tribes. The latter recognised as leaders only their hereditary *shaykhs* from the warrior aristocracy, the *djouad* and the Dawāwida,[11] and as arbiters, their marabouts or holy

---

[10] Turkish *Kuloghul*, pl. *Kuloghullari*, literally 'sons of slaves', the half-caste offspring of Turks and Algerian women, so-called because in theory the janissaries were the slaves of the Ottoman sultan. In Algerian Arabic the pronunciation is '*Kouroughli*' or '*Qourghli*'. In 1808 Boutin calculated the number of Turks at 10,000 and that of the Kouloughlis at 5,000.

[11] The term *djouad*, Ar. *ajwād*, 'the good', referred to the military aristocracy in general, that of Dawāwida, 'sons of David', to an even more distinguished nobility supposedly belonging to Quraysh, the tribe of the Prophet. The *djouad* were also called the Mahall, from Banū Maḥall, 'sons of the camp', supposedly descended from the original Arab conquerors.

men. The reputation of 'warrior Algiers' was nevertheless still high. To keep its corsairs neutral, seven countries paid regular tribute to the *deys*, while a further eight, including England, gave presents in cash or kind. The centuries-old idea of a French attack on Algiers was revived in 1827, not so much because of the decline of the Algerian state, but to resolve an embarrassing diplomatic dispute.

The Expedition of Algiers

The expedition of Algiers was not connected with the colonial policy of the Restoration Bourbon monarchy, but was a makeshift expedient for internal political consumption, carried out by a government in difficulty seeking the prestige of a military victory. Behind it lay a confused history of debts involving France, the *dey* and two Jewish merchants, which had dragged on since 1798 and culminated in 1827 with the severing of diplomatic relations when the *dey* Hussein struck the French consul and refused to apologise to this rather unsavoury businessman. France reacted by imposing a naval blockade which lasted for three years, and the *dey* retaliated with the destruction of the French trading-posts at Bône and La Calle. He sent to Constantinople for Turkish troops, although in reply the Grand Vizier dispatched only a single diplomat, Taher Pasha. After a French ship sailing under a flag of truce was fired upon in August 1829, the Polignac government was tempted by a proposal for the conquest of North Afica by the *pasha* of Egypt, Muhammad 'Ali. When this idea encountered the opposition both of the Ottoman sultan and of England, the French government resolved without enthusiasm on a 'change of plan': at the end of January it decided on military intervention. As the minister of war had written as long before as 1827, 'it would be a useful distraction from political trouble at home', and would allow the government 'to go to the country at the next election with the keys of Algiers in its hand'.

On 14 June an army of 37,000 men disembarked in the bay of Sidi Ferruch to the west of Algiers. On 19 June they repulsed an attack by the Turks reinforced by Kabyle and Arab

contingents,[12] and ten days later launched their own attack on
the so-called Emperor fort which protected Algiers. The capture
of the fort decided the fate of the city. On 5 July, the *dey* affixed
his seal to the agreement to surrender Algiers and the *casbah*
(citadel). The French commander de Bourmont guaranteed to
the 'inhabitants of all classes' respect for their liberty, their
religion, their property, their trade and their women. The fall
of Algiers caused scarcely any stir in France, except among the
businessmen of Marseilles, but it was widely reported abroad.

Before as after the success of the expedition, the Polignac
government hardly thought of keeping Algiers. Among other
ideas, it envisaged returning the Turkish militia to Asia Minor,
and 'installing in place of the *dey* a Moorish or Arab prince
at the head of a national government'. Then, in accordance
with the official instructions given to de Bourmont on 18 April,
Polignac decided on 26 June to negotiate with the Ottoman
government 'on the subject of our special interests'. Algiers and
its territory would be handed back to the Sultan in exchange
for a different piece of territory on the Algerian coast from Cape
Bougaroun to the frontier with the regency of Tunis. It was a
question of enlarging the zone of the old Africa Concessions,
the trading posts dating back to the beginning of the seventeenth
century, and occupying the city of Bône. In addition, an international conference would settle the question of 'Europe's
general interest', the suppression of piracy on the one hand and
the tributes paid by a number of countries on the other. The
capture of Algiers a few days later did not alter these plans in
any way: on 15 July de Bourmont received the order to 'take
possession of Bône, where the Genoese shipowner Schiaffino
was loading on behalf of the *Dey*'. On 17 and 19 July, Polignac
sent to the French ambassador in Constantinople finely-worded
instructions to open negotiations on the basis of the return of
Algiers in exchange for 'a slight increase in the territory over
which France has been sovereign for several hundred years',

---

[12] French generals estimated their number at 50,000; according to Si Hamdan ben Othman, a leading citizen of Algiers to whom the *Dey* turned for
assistance in the crisis, but who subsequently collaborated with the French,
there were only 30,000. The regular troops numbered 15,000; the Kabyles
were Berbers from the mountains east of Algiers, with a long history as
mercenaries.

but not to sign anything, the government 'reserving the right to accept or reject the treaty'. The ambassador to Russia was charged to inform the Tsar of the projected treaty and obtain his diplomatic support.

On the other hand, de Bourmont had drawn up a proclamation even before his departure from France, to 'the *Koulouglis*, the Arabs and the inhabitants of Algiers', declaring that the French army had come 'to drive out the Turks, your tyrants', and that they would reign as before as independent masters of their native land,[13] and thus had no intention of ceding the city to the Ottomans now that it was won. After announcing that the whole of the regency would be conquered within a fortnight, he declared first that 'the Moors and Arabs looked on us as liberators', then that he was busy 'rebuilding a government with educated and intelligent Moors', and finally that, having compromised them in this way, he was unable 'to allow them to fall back under the rule of the Turks'. To make the matter irreversible, he proceeded to expel those Turks who were settled and married in the country. As for the Bône expedition, 'there was reason to think that it would cause the *Bey* of Constantine to submit'. In short, by means of various initiatives such as a march on Blida (some miles inland from Algiers), an attempt to occupy Bougie and a landing at Oran, this first French general of Africa was intent on forcing the hand of his government in Paris.

He had no time to do so.[14] After the July Revolution of 1830, which brought down the unpopular government of King Charles X and his minister Polignac, and put an end to the Restoration Monarchy which had ruled France since the final defeat of Napoleon at Waterloo in 1815, De Bourmont offered his services to the new government of King Louis Philippe, but it forced him to relinquish his command. However, the army

[13] On 8 June, the French government, having indicated to de Bourmont its disapproval of an attack on 'the Turks in general, with whom France has remained at peace', seized all copies of this proclamation, which hardly corresponded with its policy. The general was ordered 'to say nothing which might prejudge our eventual intentions in the matter of Algiers', and a second proclamation was drawn up speaking only of war upon the Dey.

[14] The only direct testimony to Polignac's intention to keep Algiers is nevertheless that of the royalist official, Bois le Comte, long after the event.

itself had already made it clear that it did not intend to be deprived of its victory. The authority of the Turkish *odjaq* having disappeared, that of the French military was to replace it throughout the entire Regency. And indeed, for forty years from 1830 to 1870, Algeria became its parade ground and particular preserve.

Part I
ALGERIA UNDER THE MILITARY, 1830–1870

2
THE CONQUEST

French Uncertainty and 'the Time of Anarchy', 1830–34

The 'July Monarchy' of King Louis Philippe, called after the July Revolution which deposed Charles X, did not know at the outset what to do with Algiers, 'this onerous legacy of the Restoration' which had brought the kings of the Bourbon dynasty back to France after the fall of Napoleon in 1815. In June 1831 the prime minister, Casimir Périer, announced his intention to extend the French occupation to the whole of the regency, but after this there was further hesitation until 22 July 1834, the date when a government-general of the French possessions in North Africa was created. At that time these possessions were limited to the immediate environs of the coastal cities, Algiers, Oran, Bougie and Bône.

In the interval, there was general disorder throughout Algeria; for the Muslim population this was 'the time of anarchy'. In the western province of the Oranais, the tribes attacked the Turkish or *Kouloughli* garrisons while the Moroccan sultan attempted to win recognition of his suzerainty. In the central province of Titteri, the *çoffs* or tribal factions began to fight each other, while at Algiers, various notables demanded the right of self-determination and dreamed of an independent government. There was as a result no general rising against the Christian invaders.

Faced with this favourable situation from which they did not know how to profit, the generals who governed the French possessions improvised their policies according to temperament. De Bourmont's successor, General Clauzel, who was at one and the same time imperious and devious, thought that it

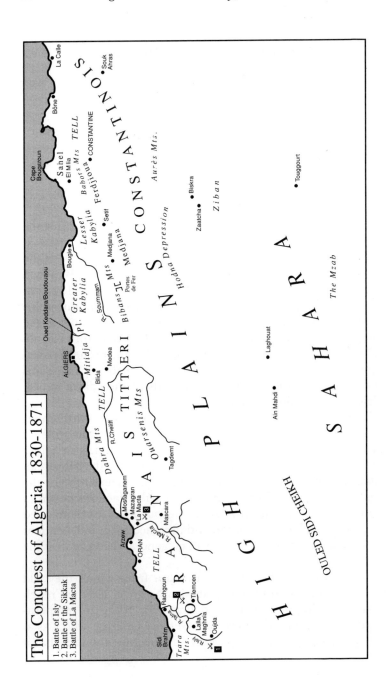

would be easy to establish French rule using Muslim chiefs as French agents. Following a plan suggested by de Lesseps, the French consul at Tunis, he proposed to install Tunisian princes as *beys* at Oran and Constantine, and to this end signed on his own authority two treaties with the ruling family of Tunis. In the first, he secretly granted the Tunisians the *beylik* of Constantine in full sovereignty.[1] In the second, he obtained the promise of a *bey* for Oran under French protection. The Turkish *bey* of Oran, overwhelmed by tribal revolt, had been effectively eliminated, while the sultan of Morocco took possession of Tlemcen. Alerted by de Lesseps, Paris recalled Clauzel, who was in danger of provoking a war with Morocco.

In his absence a sensible and reliable soldier, General Berthezène, took charge with instructions to hold back and wait. This upright officer attempted to make a reality of the protectorate over Oran, and in the Mitidja, the long, narrow plain south, east and west of Algiers, relied on a celebrated marabout or holy man who was made *agha* (commander) of the Arabs. For this he was outrageously slandered by incoming French colonists who wanted 'to drive away this mass of savages to make room for better men', as their contemporary pamphleteer Hain put it. Sébastiani, the Minister of Foreign Affairs, appointed in his place the husband of his own mistress, General Savary, Duc de Rovigo, who held the post of governor from December 1831 to April 1833. A former Minister of Police, he tyrannised the townspeople of Algiers, exterminated the Al 'Ouffia tribe, and executed Arab chiefs who were lured to Algiers by promises of safe-conduct, and at the same time came into conflict with his *Intendant Civil*, the head of the civil administration. After his death his two successors, Generals Avizard and Voirol, tried in vain to repair the damage done by his brutality. Policy at Oran was equally contradictory: General Boyer, known as Pedro the Cruel after an infamous king of old Castile, ruled the neighbourhood by terror, but his successor General Desmichels endeavoured in 1834 to turn Abd el-Kader, the rising star of

---

[1] There were two versions of this treaty. One was in French, unknown to the Tunisians, which contained a clause added by Clauzel placing the *bey* of Constantine under the authority of France. The Arabic version signed by Clauzel was not communicated to Paris.

the Arabs in the west, into his protégé as the champion of the liberation of the country from the hated Turks.

In the anarchy that submerged the country in the absence of any effective government, Muslim chiefs and notables looked for their own leaders. By 1834, two had emerged. In the east Hajj Ahmed, the *bey* of Constantine, had maintained himself in power, and claimed the succession to the *dey* as ruler of the entire country. Despite his talk of unity and agreement, he upheld his authority by force while negotiating with the French on the one hand and the Ottomans on the other. In the west it was Abd el-Kader, a young marabout of Sherifian birth belonging to the brotherhood of the Qādiriyya[2] who in 1832, at the age of twenty-four, was acclaimed by some of the tribes in the region of Mascara as 'sultan of the Arabs'. Devout and courageous, the young leader declared his first task to be the *jihād* or holy war upon the infidel, proceeding to take up residence in Mascara itself in the former palace of the *beys*. Nevertheless he accepted on 26 February 1834 the peace offered by General Desmichels.

Once again there were two treaties — one public, in French and Arabic, and the other secret, in Arabic only, which Desmichels did not communicate to Paris. By means of this subterfuge, the general was able to announce to the government the submission of the province of Oran and the freedom of trade, even though he had in fact signed an agreement by which he recognised the sovereignty of Abd el-Kader as *Amir al-Mu'minin* (commander of the faithful), the traditional title of the Caliph, and granted him a commercial monopoly at the port of Arzew, not to speak of a commitment to provide him with aid. Indeed, Desmichels went so far as to provide his ally with arms, thanks to which Abd el-Kader defeated the surviving forces of the bey of Oran on 12 July 1834. For the Muslim population it was the beginning of a new era, that of the Arab *shurafā'*.

---

[2] As his name suggests: 'Abd al-Qādir ibn Muhyi 'l-Dīn. He was the son of the man who had revived the order in western Algeria at the beginning of the century.

'The War Policy', 1835–36

Was the regency to become an Arab state? It looked as if it might from the way in which the Emir Abd el-Kader, on the pretext of crushing a fresh revolt by the rival brotherhood of the Darqāwa, disregarded the prohibitions of the new governor Drouet d'Erlon and intervened without opposition in the *beylik* of Titteri. As soon as the governor heard of the treaty with Abd el-Kader, Desmichels was replaced at Oran by General Trézel, who made alliances instead with the tribes of the former Turkish *makhzan*, or militarised tribes. Hostilities between the French and Abd el-Kader naturally resumed, culminating in the serious defeat of Trézel at the battle of the River Macta on 28 June 1835. National honour being at stake, Marshal Clauzel was sent back to Algeria in July 1835, hailed as having inherited the mantle of Scipio Africanus, the conqueror of Hannibal, the great North African enemy of the ancient Romans. All he did, however, was to multiply the resounding proclamations and the futile military expeditions. The capture of Mascara and the occupation of Tlemcen, which according to him put an end to the war, were followed by the defeat of Sidi-Yacoub and the siege of the French camp at Rachgoun. The siege was raised by an expeditionary force from France under the command of General Bugeaud, who defeated the regular troops of the Emir at the battle of the River Sikkak on 6 July 1836, then reembarked. The situation was even worse in the Mitidja, the long, narrow fertile plain in the vicinity of Algiers. The security of the city, which stands on a promontory of low hills between the western half of this plain and the sea, as well as the prospects of French settlement, depended on possession of the Mitidja, which continued to be subject to raids by the Hadjoutes, whom Clauzel had boasted that he would wipe out within two months of his arrival. At Medea, the Turkish *bey* whom he installed was made prisoner. At Bône, the Muslim adventurer Yusuf, who had made his career with the French army, alienated the tribes by his brutality; nevertheless, Clauzel believed that in this man he had the future *bey* of Constantine. He easily convinced Thiers, the prime minister, of the need to conquer the city and establish everywhere 'an absolute domination', but when Thiers was replaced by Molé in September 1836, the new government did not share the enthusiasm of Clauzel, and refused the troops required for such an expedition. In spite of everything, the hotheaded Marseillais decided to go ahead, with a force of 7,400 men at the end of November, as the rains and the first snows set in. There was not even a siege, and the retreat ended in disaster: the army lost a seventh of its men. The escapade finally discredited the *système guerroyant* or 'war policy' of Clauzel, who was replaced by General Damrémont.

The Policy of Restricted Occupation, 1837–40

The 'war policy' of Clauzel, in fact, ran counter to the policy of restricted occupation decided upon by the government in 1835. This was the policy imposed on the new governor, Damrémont, who declared himself in favour. France would limit itself to the occupation of points on the coast, namely 'Algiers, Oran and Bône, along with their hinterlands', leaving the remainder to five native chiefs, who would be vassals of France, and be kept in check by their mutual hostility. To implement this policy, Paris sent Bugeaud to negotiate with Abd el-Kader. Bugeaud himself was at that time hostile to the very idea of Algeria, 'this Bourbon affair . . . a millstone round the nation's neck, of which it would be well rid once there was the frankness and firmness to resist the little clique of squeakers in the press.' 'Like it or not', he told Thiers on 31 December 1836, 'sooner or later we'll have to get out.' In parliament, where he was a deputy, he had said 'there could be peace within six months', and he was taken at his word.

For his part, Abd el-Kader was not averse to a new Desmichels treaty, but intended to negotiate with the French as an equal, and to establish his authority over the region of Titteri. He was clever enough to make a parallel approach to the governor, Damrémont. Bugeaud, who wished to be the only 'man of peace', responded by offering concessions which Damrémont declared 'inexplicable': he gave way over the question of French sovereignty and the payment of the annual tribute, abandoned Tlemcen and their camp at the mouth of the Tafna, and conceded to Abd el-Kader the *beylik* of Titteri. In the western province of Oran, France kept only Oran itself,

Arzew, Mostaganem and Mazagran, and in the province of Algiers, apart from the city itself, only the Sahel or coastal hills on which the city stands, and part of the Mitidja plain, 'the boundary in the east to be as far as the Oued Keddara and beyond'. This strange expression, whose ambiguity, and susceptibility to differing interpretations, brought the peace to an end in 1839, meant according to Bugeaud, who had added the phrase at the end of the French text, 'to beyond the *oued* [river]'. The Arabic text of the treaty was in fact much more specific; since it fixed as the boundary the Wadī Khaḍrā' or Green River, which on reaching the Mitidja changed its name to the Boudouaou, it made clear that 'and beyond' was intended to mean the continuation of the Keddara across the plain to the sea, turning the river into a wholly unambiguous frontier. When the French text had been ratified, the prime minister felt obliged to insist that no publicity should be given to this Arabic text, which was declared lost until 1951, although in fact several copies existed. Such was the Treaty of the Tafna, 30 May 1837,[3] which recognised Abd el-Kader as the sovereign of two-thirds of Algeria, and claimed to establish peaceful coexistence between this immense Arab state and the 'two little corners' which Bugeaud had kept for France. The treaty was simply not viable, and was to be broken by both parties. Abd el-Kader entered the southern part of the province of Constantine and occupied Biskra and the Ziban; the French ceased to recognise the treaty from the day when, having at last captured Constantine, they decided to keep it. Nevertheless, the truce held for two years.

General Damrémont, for his part, had opened negotiations with the *bey* Ahmad of Constantine; he asked only for the immediate area of Bône and La Calle as French possessions, but

---

[3] Independently of the open treaty, a secret agreement was signed, whose existence was revealed to Damrémont's successor, Marshal Valée, in 1839. Bugeaud had undertaken to deliver 3,000 rifles to Abd el-Kader, to exile the chiefs of the Turkish *makhzan* tribes, and to confine the Douair tribe to a restricted territory. In return, 180,000 gold francs were to be paid to Bugeaud, of which he intended 100,000 to meet the cost of roadbuilding in his parliamentary constituency in the Dordogne. This immoral arrangement fell through, because Paris suspected the existence of secret conditions, and refused to exile the *makhzan* chiefs who had fought on the side of the French.

demanded the payment of an annual tribute of 100,000 francs. The *bey*, aspiring to the dignity of *pasha* or governor in the name of the Ottoman Sultan, and counting on the arrival of an Ottoman fleet, refused. Damrémont now received the necessary authorisation to march on Constantine and to take it 'at all costs'. The well-prepared expedition was successful; the thirty-three cannon of General Valée opened up the breaches through which the French entered the city on 13 October 1837, fighting for it house by house. Damrémont having been killed at the beginning of the battle, Valéc was promoted first to the rank of marshal and then as governor, a post which he held until December 1840.

The capture of Constantine, however, did not resolve the future of the *beylik*. At the suggestion of Molé, negotiations were reopened with the *pasha-bey*, and lasted throughout 1838. Ahmad, however, rejected the stricter terms he was offered, and continued the struggle. Valée accordingly attempted to establish a protectorate administered by the principal nobles of the Constantinois. He was opposed by General Négrier, an advocate of the strong arm and direct rule, and was obliged to replace him before introducing his own organisation, once various strategic points in the province had been occupied. Turning to the old Turkish system for inspiration, Valée entrusted the administration of the conquered *beylik* to eight notable Muslim chiefs and officials, under the authority of a French general resident at Constantine.[4] Along the coast, however, the district of Bône was placed under direct rule; four 'circles' (*cercles*) were created, each under a superior French officer assisted by a native *caid*.[5] The transfer to a civilian regime was expressly anticipated. This general arrangement, subsequently extended to the whole of Algeria, is evi-

---

[4] There were three *Khalīfas* (lieutenant-governors) for the three northern regions of the Sahel, Ferdjioua and Medjana; three great *qā'ids* (chieftains) for the three tribal confederations on the Tunisian border, the Hanencha, Harakta and Amer Cherarga; and two important figures with the rank of Khalīfa, the *ḥākim* or magistrate of Constantine and the *shaykh al-'arab*, the chief responsible for the good behaviour of the nomadic tribes.

[5] *Caid*, the French spelling of *qā'id*, commander or military chief, became the title of the principal figure in the native administration created by the French.

dence enough of the worth of Marshal Valée's political ideas. The extension of French rule made the resumption of the war with Abd el-Kader inevitable, the more so since he had profited from the truce to enlarge and organise his state. Thanks to an army of 10,000 regulars, he forced the submission of the nomads along the southern borders of the Oranais and conquered the tribes of the southern Titteri. He massacred the *Kouloughlis* of the Oued Zeitoun in the contested territory west of the Oued Kheddarā/Boudouaou, drove the fugitive Ahmad Bey from Biskra in the southern Constantinois, and razed the *ksar* (fortified village) of Ain Mahdi, the headquarters of the rival Tijāniyya brotherhood. The Emir endeavoured to unify his domains by suppressing the distinction between *makhzan* and *ra'āyā* or subject tribes with the abolition of the humiliating *kharāj* tax in favour of the *'achour*, the Qur'anic tithe.[6]

On the other hand he fought those brotherhoods like the Tijāniyya which rivalled his own, while systematically favouring the religious aristocracy of the *chorfa* or *shurafā'* at the expense of the *djouad* (military nobility). On the whole, therefore, the *djouad* fought against him. His government was essentially theocratic; he addressed his subjects as Muslims in the name of God and His Prophet. Attempts have been made to see a modernist in this perfect Believer, when he was in fact content to apply the Islamic law, and take from the Turks and the Europeans no more than their military and administrative techniques. Thus he grouped the tribes under commanders with the Turkish title of *agha*, whose district was called an *aghalik*; a number of such *aghaliks* constituted a *khalifalik*, about the size of a French *département* or old English county. By 1839 eight such *khalifaliks* had been created, divided into *aghaliks*, *caidats* and *cheikhats*,[7] but the organisation was in principle rather than practice. In military matters Abd el-Kader copied the French, building a line of depots and forts along the southern edge of the Tell, the belt of mountains running parallel to the Mediterranean between the sea and the high plains of the interior. Once again, however, although their purpose was to

---

[6] Arabic *'ushr*, 'a tenth'.

[7] The jurisdictions of a *caid* and a shaykh respectively; like the *caid* himself, both were incorporated by the French into their own administration structure.

strengthen his defences, these measures in fact amounted to little more than a statement of his objectives.

The prolongation of the truce was damaging to the religious prestige of the Commander of the Faithful, and in the belief that time was on the side of the French, from August 1839 onwards Abd el-Kader was determined to renew the holy war. The *casus belli* came at the end of October, when Marshal Valée marched from Constantine to Algiers through the defile of the Portes de Fer or Iron Gates in the Biban range. The crossing of the mountains by the only direct route between the two capitals was essential if the French were to keep control of the newly-conquered Constantinois; but the territory in question belonged to Abd el-Kader under the Treaty of the Tafna. The Emir warned Valée that he was declaring war, and eighteen days later came down to ravage the Mitidja. Valée, who had only 40,000 men, evacuated his forward positions, sent for reinforcements, and went on the offensive in the spring of 1840. But his attacks encountered nothing, since the *emir* refused direct combat. Back again as prime minister, Thiers had no further doubts about Valée's incompetence and the folly of restricted occupation. He provided for the replacement of Valée by Bugeaud as 'the only one who has beaten Abd el-Kader'.

Total Conquest, 1841–47

In complete contrast to his former views, Bugeaud was now in favour of total conquest, of 'a fight to the finish with large forces, a great invasion of Africa'. Thanks to the long government of Soult as prime minister and Guizot as minister of foreign affairs, Bugeaud remained governor-general of Algeria for nearly seven years, February 1841 to September 1847. He received all the assistance he asked for, and maintained the army in the country at a strength always above what was provided for in the budget, 83,000 in 1842 rising to 108,000 in 1846, quite apart from the various corps of native auxiliaries, some 10,000 strong. With these trumps in his hand, Bugeaud finally won; he was a first-rate commander, even if he lacked military genius. According to Pitois, he conducted 'a war of devastation', returning in effect to the system — condemned by his immediate predecessors — of expeditions in the form of *razzias* (raids) with the aim of methodically ravaging all territory not yet under French control. 'We shouldn't run after the Arabs', he said, 'but prevent them from sowing, harvesting and grazing.' From 1841, therefore, the *razzia* was 'systematically organised for the purpose of the war'. As a method of 'pacification' it seemed justified by immediate success, although in the end it only served to prolong the conflict, and resulted in the permanent alienation of the Arabs from the French.

Having destroyed the two capitals of the emir, Tagdemt (Taqdimt) and Mascara, and twice *razzia*-ed the tribes of the Hachem and the Flitta, French expeditions ravaged all the territories loyal to Abd el-Kader, and occupied all the various towns in the western Tell. Bugeaud attempted by negotiation to detach Abd el-Kader's lieutenants from their master, but failed, and was obliged to hunt them down one by one. A network of permanent posts kept conquered districts under control; another controlled the supply of grain from the north to the nomads of the south, thus keeping the borders of the desert under surveillance. After three years of struggle Abd el-Kader, at the end of his resources, was obliged to take refuge in Morocco to save what remained of his *smala* (camp), his tented capital. 'The serious warfare is over,' declared Bugeaud in July 1843, and went off in the spring of 1844 to subdue the western slopes of Kabylia, the high mountain massif to the east of Algiers which still recognised the authority of a *khalifa* appointed by the *emir*.

As he did so, however, the serious warfare referred to broke out again in the west with the arrival of Moroccan troops on the borders. The riposte was prompt and decisive; while the Prince de Joinville bombarded Tangier on 6 July, and then Mogador further south, Bugeaud's army overwhelmed the regular Moroccan army at the battle of the River Isly on 14 August 1844. The Treaty of Tangier which followed outlawed Abd el-Kader and opened the way to the definition of the frontier between Algeria and Morocco by the convention of Lalla-Maghnia, 18 March 1845. Nevertheless, in the course of that year fighting broke out once again right across the 'pacified' regions at the call of the brotherhoods. The Moroccan brotherhood of the Ṭayyibiyya provoked the insurrection of the mountain tribes of the Oranais, Titteri and the Hodna by announcing the coming of the Mahdī, the Muslim messiah under the predestined name of Muḥammad ibn 'Abd Allah, to restore the reign of Islam. In the same way, in the hinterland of the coast, the mountains of the Dahra, the valley of the Chelif and the range of the Ouarsenis were plunged into rebellion by a young *sharif* known as Bou Maaza (Goat Man). Repression was swift and severe. In the Dahra the future Marshal of France and governor-general of Algeria, Pélissier, did not hesitate to smoke to death eight hundred of the tribe of the Ouled Riah in the caves in which they had taken refuge. But Abd el-Kader reappeared in the Oranais, achieving some success around Sidi Brahim, while the tribes of the high plains to the south of the Tell and those of the Saharan Atlas on the edge of the desert revolted again at the end of the year.

This 'great insurrection' seemed to call everything back into question. Once again, large French expeditions raked, combed and subjugated the country while flying columns set off in pursuit of the elusive emir and Bou Maaza. After the rising was effectively put down in July 1846, these were forced to escape into Morocco. Returning to the Dahra in 1847, Bou Maaza was the first to surrender to the French; Abd el-Kader, attacked and expelled by Moroccan troops, did the same on 23 December 1847. With him disappeared the dream of an Arab state which he had barely the time to sketch out, but memory of which has remained fresh to the present day.

After the capitulation of the former *pasha-bey* of Constantine, Hajj Ahmad, who remained in rebellion in the Aurès mountains until 1848, only the mountain massifs of Kabylia between Algiers and Bône remained unsubdued. Inhabited by the *kabyles* (Ar. *qabā'il*, sing. *qabīla*, 'tribe'), the largest bloc of Berber-speaking peoples in the country, they were notoriously inaccessible and traditionally independent. Uncoordinated expeditions into Greater and then Lesser Kabylia in 1851 and 1853 culminated in 1857 in the decisive campaign of General Randon. Meanwhile the southern districts of the Oranais and Constantinois, once again in revolt, were declared pacified after the sieges of Zaatcha in 1848, Laghouat in 1852 and Touggourt in 1854. Algeria was henceforth conquered, if not in fact subdued.

The war, which Bugeaud called 'a *chouannerie*, a manhunt', after the rising of the royalist Breton peasants against the French Revolution in 1793, had been long, with many atrocities, and demoralising for both soldiers and officers trained to engage in acts of brutality.[8] As a result of the deficiencies of the supply corps and medical services, it proved more costly in human lives than any other colonial conquest. From the point of view of the conquered, the consequences were even worse. Their country was devastated, and its economic situation had become critical as a result of raids which were both systematic and impromptu, but above all continuous, with the raiders pillaging stores of grain, carrying off livestock and felling trees. Recurrent epidemics set in, scything down an undernourished population. The cultural damage was equally bad, and its consequences were even longer-lasting. Alexis de Tocqueville, politician and political philosopher, listed the destruction in a celebrated report to parliament in 1847: 'Everywhere we have laid our hands on these revenues [from pious foundations providing for charity or education], largely diverting them from their original purpose. We have cut down the number of charities, let schools fall into ruin, closed the colleges. Around us the lights have gone out, the recruitment of men of religion and men of the law has ceased. We have, in other words, made Muslim society far more miserable, disorganised, ignorant and barbarous than ever it was before it knew us.'

In that same report, drawn up in the name of the parliamentary commission of that year, de Tocqueville went on to declare that 'the future of our rule in Africa depends above all on the way in which we treat the natives'. It was not enough to exact submission and the payment of taxes. It was also necessary 'to think of their rights and of their needs', and to work for the development of their civilisation. 'We should not at present push them along the path of our own European civilisation, but in the direction of their own.'

---

[8] The conquest had been carried out by conscripts harshly disciplined for the purpose under a regime which in some units, the Africa Battalions and the Foreign Legion, amounted to torture. In action against the enemy, meanwhile, the worst excesses of the troops were ignored by their commanders.

The Native Policy to 1847

The proper policy towards the so-called *indigènes* (natives) long remained a subject of academic discussion as well as passionate controversy in France. Advocates of the progressive expulsion of the tribes from their lands by the spreading 'oilstain' of colonisation, theorists of coexistence and idealistic integrationists had all multiplied their own pleas and proofs without engaging the interest of either the government in Paris or the generals in Africa before 1848. 'Arab policy' was decided empirically, on the spot. To assist them in their task, the first governors instituted first of all an 'Arab *agha*', who was either Muslim or French, then an 'Arab office' (*bureau arabe*) under La Morcière (1833–4), which later became a Directorate of Arab Affairs under Pellissier de Reynaud (1837–9). This directorate was suppressed in 1839, but not before it had prompted the protectorate system adopted by Valeé in the Constantinois, as well as the division of Algeria into civil territory open to European settlement and military territory from which this was excluded.

Valée's successors were content to extend these prescriptions to the whole of Algeria as it was conquered. Bugeaud, who had begun his African career in the Oranais rather than the Constantinois and followed the example of Clauzel, at first went back to the Turkish *makhzan* system, but the new director of Arab affairs, Daumas (1841–7), who had studied Abd el-Kader's administration, converted him to the system of indirect government entrusted to Arab chiefs belonging to the military or religious nobility:[9] 'The aristocracy still have great power and influence over the natives, and must always be given great consideration.' This resort to the traditional nobility, at least to those of its members who wished to serve the French, became the rule of native policy. The difficulty was to make such turbulent vassals, especially those of the southern Oranais and Constantinois, understand that they were now no more than public servants, subject to dismissal.

[9] Such as the Ouled Mokran, the Ben Gana, the Ben Achour and the Ben Said among the warriors, and the Ouled Sidi Cheikh, Ben Ali Cherif, Ben Azzedin, Ouled Sidi 'l-Arbi and the Ouled Mubarek among the religious notables.

The military regime did not entirely abolish the previous system of government in each province; the organisation which the army had taken over from Abd el-Kader remained in place in the provinces of Algiers and Oran, as did that of the Turks in the Constantinois. Later, the Kabyles too kept their own very different institutions. Nevertheless, a single structure was imposed on the administration by the army, which divided the three main provinces, each in charge of a major-general, into 'military subdivisions' corresponding to the *khalifaliks* of Abd el-Kader, and again into circles comprising one or two *aghaliks*. The basic unit naturally remained the tribe, broken down into fractions (Ar. *firqa*) composed of a number of *douars* (groups of huts and tents). For the lesser posts of *caid* (tribal chief) and *cheikh* (head of a fraction), either notables acceptable to the people concerned or chiefs nominated by the higher-ranking *khalifas*, *bachaghas* and *aghas* were appointed. Great or small, these chiefs had the essential task of keeping control of the population and collecting the so-called *impôts arabes* or 'Arab taxes', the *achour* and the *zakāt* on grain and livestock, together with their Turkish equivalent in the Constantinois, the *hokor* or ground rent.[10] For their remuneration they received a tenth of the taxes, together with their traditional right to *corvées* or labour for ploughing, harvesting and the transport of grain.

To act as intermediaries between the French command and the native chiefs, 'bureaux of Arab affairs' were created even before the ordinance of 1 February 1844, which established a divisional administration in each province and a *bureau arabe* in each subdivision or circle. The officers and interpreters who served in them spoke Arabic and made themselves familiar with Muslim society. Living like orientals themselves, surrounded with deference and respect, they were rapidly tempted into direct administration. Bugeaud and Daumas formally refused them permission to act in this way, and instead ordered them to break up, as soon as possible, the larger commands of the native aristocracy, which the French distrusted even while they employed its members, and whose influence they

---

[10] Arabic *ḥikr*, pl. *ḥukūr*. The taxes were collected in kind until 1845, and thereafter in cash according to rates set locally by the officers commanding the circles.

persistently sought to whittle away. Nevertheless, the basic
administration of the native territories fell into the hands of the
bureaux by force of circumstance. Soldiers, administrators,
informers; judges, inspectors, technical experts; their all-round
competence inevitably turned their officers, in the eyes of the
Muslims, into the real government. Envied by other officials
of the army and administration, they immediately attracted the
implacable hatred of the first *colons* or settlers for their defence
of the tribes, as Bugeaud put it, 'against rapacity and injustice'.
The Directorate of Arab Affairs, revived under Daumas, was
accused in parliament of siding with the natives, and was duly
censured by the government.

Alongside this mixture of dominion and protectorate, for
which Daumas was fundamentally responsible, a very different
policy was followed quite naturally by civil servants and
magistrates in the limited area under civil government. Here
they behaved as if they were still in France. This practice of
assimilation of the administration of Algeria to that of France
led in 1841–2 to the creation of a French system of justice in
which only French metropolitan law was applied. Since its
jurisdiction extended to the entire population of Algeria, the
immediate result was the suppression of the criminal jurisdiction of the *cadi* or *qāḍī*, the Muslim judge, in accordance with
Islamic law. Assimilation, in fact, meant the destruction of
Muslim institutions. As a result, it became the battlecry of
colonisation.

Colonisation, 1830–47

The decade of the 1830s had been a time of unrestricted colonisation, in fact of anarchy. Immediately after the capture of
Algiers, a flight of human vultures swooped on the country,
trafficking in real estate in the cities, grabbing hold of land and
cutting down the woods. The Sahel or coastal hills of the promontory on which Algiers stands, which had been full of estates
and country houses many of which were now abandoned by
their owners, became a vacant estate where, in addition to the
khammès or sharecroppers who cultivated them,[11] dubious

[11] Arabic *khammās*; so-called because their share was a fifth of what they
produced.

European purchasers were joined by romantically-minded aristocrats, 'settlers in kid gloves', some of whom indeed became true pioneers. Clauzel himself, an ardent 'colonist' according to the theories of the day, set the example when he acquired various large properties at low prices, and set out to make the plain of the Mitidja the 'dump for Europe's beggars'. Cheap passages brought a flood of poor immigrants from Spain, the Balearic islands, Malta and Italy; Parisian labourers and German and Swiss emigrants were brought in as an official measure. The first results were poor: European agriculture did not advance as quickly as Arab cultivation retreated in the face of the first European settlements, especially since these were largely destroyed when fighting broke out anew in 1839. At that time, the European population numbered 25,000, of whom 11,000 were French.

Bugeaud, who described himself as a 'soldier-peasant', dreamed instead of collectivised colonisation by the military, but his plans were rejected. Three military settlements were founded experimentally, but all failed: the soldier-settlers, married at the drumhead to a bunch of orphan girls, chose freedom and left. Bugeaud did at least allow an aristocrat, Comte Guyot, to get on with the efficient organisation of a programme of civilian settlement directed by the state. This was based on the creation of villages and the free distribution of individual plots, at least when they had been properly brought into cultivation. The government obtained land for the purpose by appropriating the so-called public *habous* or religious property administered by the Islamic authorities for charitable purposes,[12] by sequestrating the estates of those who had fled the country, and by confiscating lands belonging to tribes that had fought against the French. At the same time the state lands of the Turkish *beylik*, together with all uncultivated land, were declared state property. Finally, a policy of systematic expropriation began to confine the tribes to ever smaller areas of their traditional territory. On this basis, with the assistance of the army, which opened up roads, built the villages and cleared the land, colonisation was a considerable success. Between

---

[12] Arabic *ḥubs*, *ḥubus*, from a root meaning 'to lock away'.

1842 and 1845, thirty-five centres were created and 105,000 hectares[13] allocated to the settlers or *colons*. Immigrants rushed in: 46,180 arrived in 1845, and there were 1,882 applications for concessions.

The ordinances of 1844 and 1846, which introduced the expropriation of uncultivated land or waste, also attempted to introduce some order into the system of landownership. But the investigation of titles to about 200,000 ha. of land amounted to little short of robbery; in the neighbourhood of Algiers, out of 168,000 ha. investigated, 95,000 fell to the state and 37,000 to individual Europeans, a mere 11,500 to Muslims. A great deal of land grazed by nomads in the course of their migrations, and other land left fallow by native agriculture, had been treated as waste; deprived of much of the land they held in joint ownership, many native communities were obliged to sell what remained and depart. The *Commission des Transactions et Partages*, dealing with such transfers and allocations, subsequently reconsidered the results of this operation, but returned no more than 22,000 ha. to the dispossessed. Thanks to the free acquisition of all this land, twenty-seven *colon* (settler) villages in the Sahel and the Mitidja were either established or extended, and by the time of Bugeaud's departure in 1847, the number of settlers implanted in the countryside had reached about 15,000 out of a total European population of 109,400, of whom 47,274 were French.

These *colons* felt sufficiently secure to want relief from military rule, but since some guarantee of French protection was essential, they looked to the state to provide it. 'It is vital', wrote one of them in 1845, 'to legislate for the incorporation of Algeria into France as an integral part of its territory. Neither the press nor the settlers themselves must rest without winning this crucial point.' And indeed, from 15 April 1845 the civil territory of Algeria, at least, was assimilated into the metropolitan system of government. Thus the ordinance of 28 September 1847 applied to this tiny area the French law of 1837 concerning the *communes*, the basic units of local government in France. The only difference was that the *maires* (mayors) appointed to the

---

[13] The hectare, abbreviation ha., a unit of measurement 100 metres square, is the basic French unit of land. 100 ha. = 1 square kilometre.

Algerian *communes* had to be paid, and their municipalities
financed, by taxpayers who were not in fact citizens, in other
words the subject Arab population. This first example shows what the colonial conception of
assimilation was. It thought only of the French and the natu-
ralised Europeans, who stood to gain additional advantages as
French citizens in the special circumstances of Algeria. From
the outset, therefore, assimilation in Algeria was designed not
only to give the French their full share of privilege, but to create
what Lyautey later called 'overblown' or super-citizens, with
rights in excess of those in metropolitan France, and far greater
than the rights of their native subjects. In France, on the other
hand, it was believed that the purpose of assimilation was first
and foremost to draw the Arabs into French civilisation, and
that the application of French laws would lead to the fusion of
the two races in the country. That is why, in accordance with
the old French ideal of universality, of French civilisation as the
way forward for the whole of mankind, both government and
public opinion were on the whole favourable to the claims made
by the colonists on behalf of the integration of the colony into
metropolitan France. This fundamental mistake as to the true
meaning of assimilation in the country lasted throughout the
whole history of French Algeria.

3

ALGERIA UNDER THE SECOND REPUBLIC AND THE SECOND EMPIRE, 1848–1870

A First Taste of Assimilation: The Second Republic, 1848–51

To the *colons* the Revolution of 1848, which overthrew the 'July Monarchy' of Louis-Philippe and replaced it with a republican government, the second since the great French Revolution of 1789, brought the hope of an end to military rule and the introduction of complete assimilation. It was therefore warmly welcomed. Although the reality was different, and the generals of Africa remained all-powerful in Paris, the settlers in fact received considerable satisfaction.[1] The institution of universal suffrage enabled the French in Algeria to send four deputies to the Constituent Assembly and three to the Legislative Assembly, and gave them the right to elect municipal councillors. At the same time, non-French Europeans and the Muslims who lived in the new French *communes* also received the right to elect representatives to the municipal council up to a third of its membership. However, this metropolitan refinement was abandoned in 1850 at the insistence of the civilians of Algiers, who considered the natives 'hardly worthy of the right to vote' and demanded 'a special regime' for them in which the laws of France would not apply.

The Constitution of 1848 declared Algeria to be an integral part of France, and promised that it would be subjected to the laws of the metropole. And indeed, an attempt was made to bring about the *rattachement* or direct affiliation of the main branches of the civilian administration — religion, education, justice and customs — to the corresponding ministries in Paris. By the terms of a decree of 9 December 1848, the civil territories of the Algerian provinces — i.e. those limited areas which had

---

[1] Quite apart from assimilation, the *colons* claimed the right to rule Algeria themselves. In 1848 they convened an elected Algerian Congress which set out to discuss 'all political and financial matters affecting Algeria'.

been placed under civilian as distinct from military administration — became three *départements*, the basic units of provincial administration in France, each divided into *arrondissements* (districts) and subdivided into *communes*, the whole administered in metropolitan fashion by prefects, sub-prefects and mayors. By-passing the governor-general, the prefects corresponded directly either with the relevant ministries or with the Algerian department at the ministry of war. But the *conseils généraux* or county councils which had been promised for the new *départements* did not materialise before 1858. Moreover, the former 'mixed' and 'Arab' territories were not only regrouped under the name of 'military territories' but remained in the hands of their military commanders, maintaining the former system of indirect administration through the *bureaux arabes* and the local chiefs, even though the Directorate of Arab Affairs, which had been execrated by the *colons*, was finally abolished. In spite of the conflicts and quarrels which it produced at first between the generals and the prefects in charge of the civil territories, this dual system survived intact until June 1858, basically because the civil servants gave way before the so-called 'big epaulettes' of the army.

The Second Republic intended to deal with the problem of property rights in Algeria by assimilating them to those of France. But the bill drawn up in Algiers pretended rather too cleverly that private property did not exist in Algeria as a result of the original Arab conquest, which according to Islamic law would have made the state the owner of the land, and the tribes merely collective tenants. The Assembly in Paris did not dare take a final decision, but set aside the provision which gave the state the ownership of tribal land in the absence of title deeds. Wishing to maintain the previous system of land ownership, it decided that land in native ownership was of two kinds: private property, subsequently called by the Islamic legal term '*melk*' (*milk*), and collective ownership, which came to be called '*arch*', from the Arabic *'arsh* or tribe. This last was a category quite unknown to the people concerned, whose property was not collective but simply undivided. In other words, it was not permanently parcelled out among the individuals who cultivated and grazed it. The law did declare that the state was the owner of all forest land, while recognising existing rights of usage, but these were defined according to the French Forest Laws of 1827, which did not allow for the fact that the woods and scrublands of Algeria were essentially pasture. When the French code was strictly applied and the forests were delimited, the native pastoralists were either expelled from their traditional domain or remained there in breach of the law.

The colonisation of Algeria remained the major concern. In the aftermath of the workers' uprising in Paris in June 1848, the Second Republic felt itself called upon to solve the underlying social problem, and the Assembly voted 50 million francs to clear the capital of subversive elements. Unemployed artisans and labourers made over 100,000 applications for free grants of land in Algeria; in the end there were 20,000 such emigrants, 15,000 of them from Paris, who settled in Algeria in forty-two new villages. Left to themselves in impossible circumstances, these makeshift *colons*, most of whom knew nothing of farming (one was 'terribly afraid of his ox'!), endured hardships which were to no avail; within a short space of time 3,000 were dead, while 7,000 returned to France. Other villages built by the new *départements* fared a little better. Nevertheless at the end of 1851, there were 33,000 rural colonists out of 131,000 Europeans (66,000 of them French). Against the 'old *colons*' of the towns, it was the agricultural village settlements which assured the success of Napoleon's nephew Louis-Napoléon Bonaparte in the plebiscite of December 1851, when 53.46 per cent of the Algerian electorate voted for the new President who had just overturned the government of the Second Republic in a populist coup backed by the generals. If the military vote is included, 65.96 per cent voted yes; by the time of the referendum which approved the creation of the Second Empire in November 1852, almost everyone had come round to the Bonapartist cause, with 89 per cent in favour of the transformation of the President into the Emperor Napoleon III.

The reforming zeal of the outgoing Republic had roused the Muslim notables to protest against the Schoelcher decree of 1848, emancipating the mainly black slaves of Algeria who provided the rich with domestic servants, and the decree consequently was not applied with great rigour. For the Muslim population in general, however, the period was marked above all by the major epidemics which characterised 'the years of misery', 1845–51. The economic crisis of 1847–51, which affected the settlers, hit the *fellahs* or native peasants far harder after three years of drought and locusts. Bad harvests and dwindling flocks, as well as 'frightful famines' here and there, explain why the outbreaks of cholera in 1849–51 had such lethal effect. In 1851 the native population numbered no more than 2,324,000, excluding some 190,000 in the still unconquered regions of Kabylia.

The Algeria of Randon and the bureaux arabes, 1852–58

From 1852 to 1858 the military once again enjoyed their freedom to govern Algeria as they pleased. They were supported by a government which had risen to power with the assistance of the army, unhindered by the settlers who had lost their right to elected representation in Algeria as well as Paris Assisted by the return of prosperity, they governed with considerable success. The Muslim population gave the credit to the *Bureaux arabes* and to the governor-general, Randon.

Marshal Randon himself was much concerned with the programme of colonisation. An advocate of small-scale settlement, 'which cultivates with its hands, builds with its pennies, and puts down roots for a generation destined to live off the land', he encouraged immigration and the building of villages, fifty-six of which were built between 1853 and 1859, while the agricultural population increased by about 15,000. To obtain the necessary land, he followed his predecessors' practice of restricting certain tribes to a fraction of their former territory, a policy henceforth known as *cantonnement* ('delimitation'), on the analogy of the forestry practice of the same name. *Indigènes* — natives who were classified as the owners of simple rights of usage of the *arch* or tribal territories they inhabited — were invited to cede to the state domain those lands which they did not need; in return, the state recognised their individual or collective ownership of the lands it allowed them to keep. The procedure of *cantonnement*, carried out on simple local instructions, has not always left its mark in the documentation but, as far as one can tell, from 1851 to 1861 it affected sixteen tribes and 343,387 ha., of which 61,363 came to the state. Randon nevertheless perceived that the operation was turning into *refoulement*, i.e. the driving away of the tribes from the region of colonisation altogether; and when he eventually took charge of Algerian affairs in Paris as Minister of War in the 1860s, he opposed its general extension.

To counterbalance the development of assisted colonisation, the governor also set out to encourage private enterprise and the influx of capital. Private colonisation made remarkable progress. In 1856, the province of Constantine contained more settlements due to individual initiative than farms cultivated by official settlers. Financial institutions were attracted by the opportunity to obtain vast properties from the state against the promise to develop them by building new villages for fresh *colons*, although as a rule they did not fulfil their undertakings. A group of Swiss financiers, for example, obtained the freehold of 12,340 ha. around Sétif in this way, but after bringing in 2,956 immigrants, the Compagnie Génévoise went back on its promises, expelled its settlers, and contented itself with the profits from Muslim sharecropping. Nevertheless, in ten years 50,000 ha. were given to fifty-one companies, as against 250,000 ha. for small-scale individual settlement. As a result, the rural element in the European population reached 83,000 out of a total of 189,000. From 1856 onwards, the birthrate of this population was always higher than the death-rate, and it was clear that a true settler colony and not just some plantation system had been founded.

However, it was still necessary to make this colony economically viable. The almost complete suppression of customs barriers between France and Algeria in January 1851, the founding of the Bank of Algeria in August of that year, and the establishment of a Commodities Exchange in April 1852 encouraged economic growth. Originally it had been thought that Algeria would become a supplier of tropical commodities. Cotton, introduced after 1850 to meet the 'cotton famine', prospered until 1867 but then collapsed. Tobacco and plants for perfume were successful over a much longer stretch of time. But the *colons* soon realised that the most profitable form of agriculture was cereal-growing, which remained vital until the great spread of the vine in the 1880s. The economic infrastructure was actively developed: a network of roads was constructed, and in April 1857 it was decided to build a railway system. The first great dams were built and drainage works undertaken, notably in the Mitidja.

The *bureaux arabes*, the real rulers of the tribes during this period, who rewarded them with the name *makhaznya* (men of the government), tried to associate the Muslim population with this economic progress.[2] They wished to settle the nomadic pastoralists and cultivators to create a firmly-rooted peasantry of smallholders who would owe the security of their titles to France. For this reason they blocked the policy of *cantonnement* and undertook what amounted to their own programme of colonisation by establishing native villages and putting up houses and various other buildings like caravanserais and *fondouks* (Ar. *funduq*), inns and hostels for travellers and merchants. They endeavoured to overcome malaria and generally to improve the native economy. Thus they introduced European agricultural implements and new crops such as cotton, potatoes and tobacco, developed the cultivation of vines. figs and olives, favoured the protection of woodland, and encouraged sheep-rearing with the construction of shelters and watering-places and the use of hay. In spite of their lack of means, the feebleness of indigenous resources and the innate conservatism of poor peoples, their efforts were not entirely fruitless. It goes without saying that established ways of life, adapted over the centuries to the environment, were not fundamentally changed. Nevertheless, the use of hitherto unknown techniques and crops and the discovery of new resources with the gathering of esparto grass and the opening-up of mines, all amounted to a distinct gain. Certainly, the economic prosperity of the years 1851–57 benefited the *fellahs* considerably; good prices made the cultivation of wheat and barley highly profitable, and led to an increase in the land under cereals. At the same time, however, the growth of dependence upon the market in grain, livestock and wool, together with the payment in cash

[2] The *Bureaux arabes* numbered about forty, rising to forty-nine in 1870, with some 150 officers increasing to 206 in 1866. Allowing for the personnel attached to each bureau: a doctor, an interpreter, a *khodja* or native secretary, two secretarial assistants, a *chaouch* or native sergeant and a variable number of *spahis* and *mokhaznis* or native troops, it could be said that Algeria was held by 1,500 to 2,000 men, plus six or seven hundred *caids* appointed by the state.

of higher taxes, led to a considerable expansion of money-lending. With the economic crisis of 1857–8, the fall in the price of cereals and the catastrophe of 1867–8, the previous progress came to nothing.

It was during this period at the beginning of the Second Empire that Muslim justice was organised along modern lines with *mahakmas* (Ar. *mahkama*, pl. *mahākim*) or courts in which the *cadi* (the Muslim judge) judged in the first instance, while appeals went to tribunals called *medjles* (Ar. *majlis*, pl. *majālis*). This free and speedy form of justice, in which only Muslim *oukils* (Ar. *wakīl*. pl. *wukalā'*) or attorneys could represent the parties was welcomed by the natives subject to their jurisdiction. However, along with all the other quite remarkable efforts of government at the time, it was considered inadequate by *colon* opinion. Lawyers deprived of their native clientele joined in the complaints and protests of the *petits colons* or smallholders — suffering from the meagre size of their allotments — whom the Republican opponents of the Empire incited against the 'Regime of the Sword'. The Doineau affair, in which the head of the *bureau arabe* of Tlemcen was condemned to death for the killing of an *agha* in his district, brought matters to a head. The lawyer Jules Favre turned the trial into that of the *bureaux arabes* themselves, and of the military administration in general. Waged in the name of assimilation into metropolitan France, the campaign against the *'bourreaux d'Arabes'* or 'executioners of the Arabs' swayed French public opinion. In June 1858, yielding to the settlers' demands, Napoleon III put an end to military rule.

A Fresh Experiment with Assimilation: The Ministry of Algeria, 1858–60

Ten years after the first experiment with administrative and political assimilation, a second and more radical trial was made over a period of two years, with far-reaching consequences. With the exception of education and religion, which were attached to the corresponding ministries in Paris, all branches of the administration were brought together in a Ministry of Algeria and the Colonies. The Government-general and consultative committee were suppressed, and the colony was entrusted to a minister resident in Paris, none other than the Emperor's young cousin, Prince Napoléon-Jérôme. A self-proclaimed democrat, anti-clerical as well as anti-militarist, the Prince wished to treat Algeria, which he had never seen, as a simple extension of France, 'ruling from Paris and administering on the spot' in accordance with French principle and practice. The extent of civil territory was immediately doubled and six new sub-prefectures were created, together with five civil commissions in military territory. The *conseils-généraux* or councils for the three *départements*, nominally established by the Second Republic, at long last saw the light of day.[3] The new regime, denouncing the incompetence and 'excesses' of the military administration, created so-called disciplinary commissions to take over the task of policing the native population hitherto carried out by the *bureaux arabes*, and made use of a series of civilian *bureaux arabes* — which seem to have been generally incapable. At the request of the settlers, restrictions on property transactions were lifted in February 1859, while a decree was prepared governing the *cantonnement* of tribal lands.

Assimilation was, in effect, to be extended to the Muslim population. 'We are', wrote the new minister on 31 August 1858, 'confronted by a hardy perennial, a strongly-rooted national identity which must be eradicated by assimilation.' He did not disguise the fact that his purpose was 'the breakdown and dissolution of the Arab nation'. The idea was to cut down the native aristocracy, weaken the authority of the *caids*, and 'take the tribe to pieces', in particular by encouraging the breaking of ties between landowners and sharecroppers. Some of the latter took advantage of the opportunity to leave their traditional lords without paying their debts, and came for hire by the *colons* in civil territory where they were exempt from the *impôts arabes*, the so-called 'Arab taxes'.[4] The result was disruption of the native economy and especially of the traditional ties of mutual assistance, the effects of which were severely felt in 1867.

[3] Their members were nominated, not elected, but they discussed the budget, and were concerned with military as well as civil territory.
[4] See above, p.23

The same policy was maintained by the Prince's successor, Chasseloup-Laubat, who took office as minister in March 1859. He did away with the 1854 reorganisation of Muslim justice, breaking down the exclusive character of the *mahakma* and the *medjles* by giving the Arabs the right of appeal to French courts. The faithful refused to have anything to do with such apostasy, and strongly resented the attack on their religion. Almost all felt threatened by the triumph of the *colons* and became restive; some chiefs or landowners preferred to emigrate to countries where Islam was still supreme.

The *bureaux arabes* and the military remained opposed to the new regime, and endeavoured to open the Emperor's eyes to the damage being done by a policy which dangerously disturbed the indigenous society. Thus alerted, Napoleon III came to Algiers himself in September 1860 to make his own inquiries. He was in fact already convinced that Algeria should not be handed over to the settlers. 'The question of Algeria has veered off course since the day it was called a colony', he said; France's first duty was to attend to the welfare of three million Arabs. The announcement heralded a total change of policy. A decree of 26 November 1860 abolished the Ministry of Algeria, to the consternation of the *colons*.

During the brief period of the Ministry's existence, however, the *colons* had gained far more than a further seventeen settler villages and an additional 4,600 free concessions. Politically they had triumphed. In the *conseils généraux*, the councils of the three *départements*, they had at their disposal a platform from which to level the worst accusations against the *bureaux arabes*, 'this anti-French bunch'. Meanwhile, an administrative experiment in which France no longer maintained a balance of some kind between the two populations had done more than disturb and antagonise Muslim society. It had reopened the era of insurrection. If the rising in the Aures in 1859 was not the direct consequence, that of the Hodna in 1860 was officially ascribed to fear of *cantonnement* and the inroads into Muslim justice. In the same way, although the rebellion of the great tribe and brotherhood of the Ouled Sidi Cheikh in 1864 had specific causes, its extension from the desert fringes into the Tell was the result of the panic created among Muslim chiefs by the policies of the Ministry of Algeria and the *cantonnement* of the tribes. The ferment in the Oranais, the Tell and the Dahra and among the Beni Menacer spread beyond Algiers into Kabylia, especially the eastern districts. Reinforcements were necessary to keep control of the country and to quell the rebellion, the worst since 1845. But the *colons*, far from accepting responsibility, accused the military of provoking the uprising in order to make themselves indispensable.

The Algerian Policy of Napoleon III

In these circumstances, the decision of the Emperor in December 1860 to reestablish the previous military regime with increased powers for the governor becomes more understandable. Although a few services continued to be directed from Paris, government and administration were once again concentrated in Algiers in the hands of a governor-general assisted by a military lieutenant-governor, a government council and a *conseil supérieur*. It was unfortunate that the new governor-general, the aged Marshal Pélissier, who since the infamous affair of the Dahra (p. 20) had gained renown in the Crimean war, should take no interest in the administration. The Director-general of civil affairs, Mercier-Lacombe, took the opportunity to push for the legalisation and extension of *cantonnement*. But Napoleon III, who in contrast had asked for 'something to be done for the Arabs', would not have his hand forced in this way. He said: 'It is above all necessary to guarantee to the natives respect for their lands and their rights.' The army officers and the civilian theorists of a policy of *association* with the Muslims, men like Generals Fleury and Morris, Colonels Lapasset and Gandil, the prefect Frédéric Lacroix and the government adviser Thomas-Ismaïl Urbain (a convert to Islam) convinced the Emperor that the politically and economically anachronistic policy of rural colonisation was the wrong road to follow: 'The real Algerian peasant is the native',[5] and European immigrants should stay in the towns,

[5] Urbain forecast that 'the liquidation of agricultural colonisation would come about of its own accord. It will lead on the one hand to industrial agriculture and market gardening, and on the other to the progressive replacement of the immigrants by the natives in all outlying areas.'

concerned only with commerce and industry. The development of the country could only be accomplished through the *association* of Arabs and Europeans refereed by the government on the spot. Napoleon III expressed his wishes in the famous letter to Pélissier of 6 February 1863, in which he took up these arguments.

The letter aroused the fury of the *colons*, who seized provocatively upon the single sentence: 'Algeria is not, strictly speaking, a colony but an Arab kingdom.' Various historians who have espoused their cause have been driven by the statement to condemn this anti-colonial policy as an attempt 'to reconstitute a national Arab identity', whereas the Emperor himself, in agreement with the military, was simply anxious 'that Algeria should be a source of strength and not weakness for France. For this to happen, the smoothing down of confrontation and the agreement of interests are indispensable.' He wanted to see 'perfect equality between natives and Europeans' and reconciliation between the races: 'The natives like the *colons* have an equal right to my protection.' To reassure the native population, the *sénatus-consulte* or Imperial act of 22 April 1863 pronounced 'the tribes of Algeria owners of the lands which traditionally they have always enjoyed'.

Neither the declared opposition of old Pélissier, who came close to being removed from office before his death in 1864, nor the native rebellion of 1864 made Napoleon III abandon his Algerian policy. This so-called waverer made a long investigative tour in May 1865, and reiterated to the Muslims: 'France is not here to destroy the national identity of a people . . . I want to increase your wellbeing, draw you increasingly into the administration of your country and the benefits of civilisation.' He requested the *colons* to whom he announced a grant of 100 million francs for public works, to treat the Arabs 'as compatriots'. On 20 June 1865 the Emperor made known his instructions to Governor Mac-Mahon, although their publication was delayed in Algeria, so offensive were they to colonial prejudices. He ordered an end to the war upon the natives waged by the state domain and the forestry commission. Efforts were rather to be directed to providing those tribes which had been unjustly despoiled with an equivalent amount of land. Native property would be exempt from seizure for debt incurred before 1863. Muslims should become French citizens while retaining their separate status under Islamic law. The Emperor also recommended the restoration of Muslim justice, the development of public education, the opening of Muslim secondary schools, and an increase in the numbers of native regiments; in short, protection, reconciliation, association.

In setting out his policy in this way, Napoleon III was drawing directly and in detail upon the letters of Colonel Lapasset. His plan broke sharply with the policy of assimilation in Algeria, 'sententiously advanced to assimilate the Arab population, but having no other result than its exploitation, and the sacrifice of its most cherished institutions to our interests'. The immediate outcome was the *sénatus-consulte* of 14 July 1865, which established the Muslims of Algeria as French, the equals of those with their roots in metropolitan France. While preserving their *statut personnel* or personal status, in other words their rights and obligations under Islamic law, Muslims would henceforth be able to enter both civil and military employment. They would also be able to request their 'naturalisation', i.e. their full rights as French citizens, but only if they were willing to abandon their *statut personnel* as Muslims and accept French law in matters such as marriage and inheritance. Similar provisions were made for the Algerian Jews, who lived under their own Rabbinic law. But the requirement to abandon their status under Islamic or Jewish law meant in effect that neither Muslims nor Jews applied for the full citizenship on offer.[6]

The two *sénatus-consultes* of 1863 and 1865 put an end to the uncertainty regarding the status of property and persons so far as the natives of Algeria were concerned, while the Emperor's policy opened up the prospect of a promising future for the peoples of Algeria. The Algerian *colons* thought otherwise. As General Hanoteau, an officer of the *bureaux arabes*, put it: 'What our settlers dream of is a bourgeois feudalism in which they will

---

[6] Between 1865 and 1875 only 371 Muslims were 'naturalised', and between 1865 and 1870 only 142 Algerian Jews. It was to get round this Jewish reluctance that a decree of collective naturalisation was prepared at the instance of Jewish members of the French Assembly, anxious to place the Jews of Algeria on the same footing as themselves. Emile Ollivier sent it to the *Conseil d'Etat* or Cabinet in March 1870. Crémieux, who gave his name to the decree when it was passed in October 1870, simply promulgated the text.

be the lords and the natives the serfs.' They mounted a determined campaign against 'the Emperor of the Arabs'. Algiers
took to the barricades, 'Defence Committees' were set up, and
petitions circulated containing the words 'Do you want to be
Frenchmen or Arabs?' The Algerian press, its articles reprinted
in the opposition press in France, aired all the *colons'* grievances,
which were taken up in parliament. The Emperor was sacrificing French nationals by invoking the rights of the natives: he
was biased in favour of some national Arab identity while
despising the 'Kabyle people', the Berber language group of
'noble' natives, and was recreating the Arab feudal aristocracy
at the expense of humble peasants. The subtlest argument was
that his policy prevented the development of native society by
isolating it from the *colons*, one that has deceived historians
down to the present day.

In fact, the Emperor's policy was quite clearly intended to
promote the evolution of the Muslim population and not to
fossilise their patriarchal, tribal society. The *sénatus-consulte* of
1863 envisaged the creation of districts called *douars-communes*
or native local authorities, Arab communes-to-be equipped
with *djemaas*[7] — assemblies or councils for the discussion of
affairs — and to replace the anachronistic framework of the
tribe. As a temporary measure, 'subdivisional *communes*' were
created at the level of the military subdivisions of each province, to group together the newly-established *douars* and the
tribes still unaffected by the reorganisation. Finally, in between
those *communes* which were purely Arab and those which were
properly French, *communes mixtes* ('mixed communes') were
invented, in which the commanding officer of the *cercle* would
act as mayor while a municipal committee of Europeans, Jews
and Muslims would assist the introduction of the natives into
the French system, bringing about 'the association of communities'. These *communes mixtes* were eventually to become
communes de plein exercice, fully-fledged metropolitan communes
like those already introduced into the civil territory of Algeria
where, to crown the whole of this grand reorganisation of local
government, they had been emancipated from the restrictions
of military rule. Under the new arrangement native, foreign

[7] Arabic *jamā́a*, pl. *jamā́āt*.

European and French municipal councillors sat together for the conduct of their joint affairs, the French representation being two-thirds of the total; meanwhile Muslim representatives were to be elected to the *conseils généraux* or departmental councils under the terms of a decree of June 1870.

Muslim justice likewise was reorganised yet again. In 1866, special mixed Franco-Muslim divisions of the Court of Appeal replaced the *medjles* or panels of Muslim jurists which since 1859 had been restricted to rendering advice on points of Islamic law. An Upper Council of Muslim Law now became responsible for its interpretation. It is clear that the policy in question, which has been woefully misunderstood, deserves a very different name from that of 'the Arab kingdom' by which it is still known. One of those responsible, Thomas-Ismaïl Urbain, described it more accurately in his Saint-Simonian vocabulary as 'a policy of civilisation for the Algerians'[8] — or, in modern terms, a genuine policy of association.

Combatted by the civil administration, Napoleon's policy was actively supported by the *bureaux arabes*, even though after 1858 the disheartening of the better officers had diminished their zeal and turned many of them, as the Arabs said, into '*bureaux d'administration*'. For all that, the military in general practised a policy of *rapprochement*, of bringing the communities together, so that in 1871 Jules Favre, the hostile prosecutor of the military regime in the Doineau affair, was anxious to rectify the judgements he had expressed in 1857: 'It is to the eternal honour of the officers of the *bureaux arabes* that they have discovered how to become and to remain the friends of the natives.' The Islamic religion benefited from a genuine consideration which showed itself in new religious building, the restoration of the right of pilgrimage to Mecca, the respect paid to Muslim religious dignitaries, and the prohibition of Christian missions. Regarding the religious brotherhoods, the *bureaux arabes* showed themselves as intelligent as they were skilful,

---

[8] The Saint-Simonians and their philosophy of progressive social engineering by the enlightened combination of modern technology, economic expertise and state direction, had been influential since the 1830s and 1840s, taking a particular interest in exporting their ideas to North Africa and Egypt. They came into their own under the Second Empire, when their ideas were extensively translated into government policy, not least in Algeria.

neutralising any hostility by setting the leaders against each
other, and favouring the local heads or *moqaddems*[9] together
with the shaykhs of the *zāwiyas* or lodges[10] at the expense of the
masters of the orders to which they belonged.

Alarmed to see the native population sinking into ignor-
ance, the *bureaux arabes* set out to restore the system of Muslim
education which had been destroyed by war, expropriation and
the emigration of teachers. 'Elementary instruction', wrote
Pellissier de Reynaud, the father of the *bureaux arabes*, in 1836,
'is at least as widespread among them as among us. There are
schools for reading and writing in most villages and *douars*.'
The confiscation of property belonging to the mosques dried
up especially the resources for teaching in the *médersas*[11]
(colleges), which were attended by 'two or three thousand
young people in each province'. Of these, 'six to eight hundred
by province went on to the study of *fiqh* [legal science] and
theology', and to qualify for the title of *'ulamā'* (sing. *'ālim* —
scholars). To make good the damage done to this traditional
structure, elementary Koranic schools were reopened in military territory (they numbered 2,000 in 1863), while 'Arab-
French' primary schools were introduced in the towns and
among certain tribes, teaching Arabic in the morning and
French in the afternoon. Since these were made the responsibility of *communes* — which refused them funds —, such
schools, of which there were thirty-six in 1870, had to be sub-
sidised and defended against closure. To train the teachers,
an *école normale* (teacher-training college) was established at
Algiers in 1865, with twenty French and ten Muslim student
teachers. In each *commune* the French schools themselves were
open to Arab children, although they did not attend. With a
whole generation lost to schooling, it was thought that initially
secondary education should be spread 'among the upper
classes, from which it would descend to the masses'. The first
Franco-Arab college was therefore created at Algiers in 1857,
followed by two others at Constantine and Oran respectively.
A native school of arts and crafts was opened at Fort-Napoléon

---

[9] Arabic *muqaddam*, 'one placed in charge'.
[10] See above, n. 8.
[11] Arabic *madrasa*, 'place of study'.

in Kabylia in 1867. Finally, for the learned professions of *adoul*[12] (notary), *oukil*[13] (attorney), *cadi*, *mufti* (jurisconsult) and college professor, three *médersas* were restored and modernised. This very considerable effort was criticised on the pretext that Muslim pupils were 'being educated separately in special institutions'. However, what the *colons* in fact saw in such institutions was a particularly dangerous example of Arabophilia.

Imperial policy restrained the expansion of rural colonisation, on which a maximum limit was imposed. Nevertheless, between 1861 and 1864 the administration did create eleven new villages, followed by eleven more in 1870, granting 116,000 ha. of land and installing 4,580 new settlers. In these ten years the rural European population rose from 86,000 to 118,000. To attract serious settlers with some capital of their own, free concessions were abolished in December 1864 in favour of sales at a fixed price. Now that they had become French, the natives too could buy in this way, but most of the land on offer was bought by French companies. In addition, 160,000 ha. of cork-oak forest were acquired under advantageous conditions by concessionary developers. These forests, leased at first by the state, were devastated by successive fires. The leaseholders therefore obtained from the Ollivier government in 1870 the free transfer of the burnt areas into their possession, and a third of what was left, 78,453 ha. in all. The remaining 84,623 ha. they then bought for 5,077,400 frs., an average purchase price of 31 frs. per hectare against an annual yield of 23 frs.

The help of the great private con.panies was equally sought to finance the building of the economic infrastructure. For the construction of major public works, these companies took possession of vast tracts of land belonging to the state, but did not always fulfil their contracts. Thus the Société Générale Algérienne, which undertook to spend 100 million frs. on such works and to lend a further 100 million, received 100,000 ha., of which 89,500 were *'azel*[14] land in the Constantinois. But by

[12] Arabic *'adl*, pl. *'udūl*.
[13] Arabic *wakīl*, pl. *wukalā'*.
[14] *'Azel*, Ar. *'azl*, denoted a form of contract whereby the Turkish regime had leased state lands on a revocable basis.

1870 it had paid into the scheme only 75 million frs., which eventually rose to a maximum of 87 million, and spent perhaps 27 million. It did, admittedly, open credit houses which discounted bills worth 528 million frs. Right down to the end of the colonial period, the settlers who profited from the credit and the public works continued to demand that the 100,000 ha. in question, which were leased mainly to the *fellahin* (native peasantry), be allotted to colonisation. Despite such shortcomings, the commitment of the state to great public works attracted 50,000 more Europeans into Algeria, and the economic infrastructure of roads, ports, dams and reservoirs which it created made possible the rapid extension of colonisation after 1871.

The Crisis of the 1860s and the Parliamentary Empire

A series of natural catastrophes in the late 1860s brought into question all the efforts of the past twenty years. The combined effects of swarms of locusts in 1866, of animal epidemics and years of drought, resulted in a terrible famine in the interior of the country from November 1867 till June 1868. Ever since cereals had been commercialised, the traditional granaries had been abandoned, thus depriving Algeria of its reserves; there was no experience to bring the necessary large-scale relief in time, and some 300,000 natives died of hunger, typhus and cholera.[15] The military administration and the 'Arab empire' were held responsible. An agricultural commission of inquiry toured Algeria in 1868. The *colons* blamed 'Arab communism', and gave as the cure the general introduction of freely marketable individual property. Their spokesmen gave their reasons: 'Once private property is established in the tribe, Europeans will quickly find their way in. They will find there the lands they need and the manpower they lack.' On the

---

[15] The official death-toll was 215,603 in nine and a half months, but the administration later recognised that this figure was an underestimate. The newspapers spoke of 5–600,000 dead. The Muslim population, which was estimated at 2,652,000 in 1866 was estimated at 2,125,000 in 1872 and 2,462,000 in 1876, which indicates that the figure for 1872 is incorrect.

political front, they renewed their call for a civilian administration and assimilation.

In 1869 the government tried to regain the initiative by endowing Algeria with a constitution which 'would seek to reconcile the aspirations of the settlers with the interests of the natives'. Previous proposals for a constitution of this kind, opposed to total assimiliation, had been put forward in 1852 and 1861-2, but these were now abandoned in favour of a new plan adopted in March 1870. This — the Randon-Béhic constitution, named after the two men who drew it up — envisaged an Algeria divided into civil and 'native' departments, with control over its own budget and governed by its own minister resident in Algiers. Muslims would have been represented in all local assemblies right up to a *conseil supérieur* elected by the *conseils généraux* to consider the budget. A government amendment would have gone so far as to admit them to the election of deputies to Paris. The *colons*, on the other hand, remained opposed to any idea of a special constitution 'so as not to be separated from the Motherland', and called instead for the allocation of native tax-payers to the French *communes*, and for the 'recovery of lands abandoned [to the Arabs] by the *sénatus-consulte* [of 1863]'. In Paris their representatives condemned the project as 'autonomist' and the political liberties granted to the Muslims as 'injurious to the French population'. On 9 March 1870 they won a unanimous vote in favour of the introduction of the full French civil regime.

In this way the French parliament expressed the deep-rooted feeling of those who thought, along with the nationalist writer Prevost-Paradol, that 'it was necessary to bring in laws designed exclusively to favour the expansion of the French colony, leaving the Arabs thereafter to fight as best they could, on equal terms, in the battle of life'. Lannes de Montebello, who had become a *colon*, put it even more explicitly: 'What could be more legitimate than to oblige the convenience of 2,500,000 Arabs to give way to the higher interests of 40 million French?' The settlers' victory was consolidated by the new parliamentary regime introduced by Napoleon III in April 1870 and overwhelmingly approved by the referendum of 8 May.[16] The

[16] The French of Algeria registered a protest vote: 53.6 per cent against and

incoming Ollivier government favoured them with a decree which provided for 'the individual allocation of native land in undivided ownership'. This meant the introduction of private property rights into tribal territories hitherto legally protected against the encroachments of European settlement. Muslim chiefs saw the decree as heralding the dissolution of native property and native society, and openly declared that they would not accept 'settler rule'. The *colons* did not care, convinced that 'the Arabs no longer had the strength or the capacity to revolt'.

42.9 per cent in favour. The votes of the army and the navy were counted together; in Algeria they gave 16.6 per cent against and 83 per cent in favour, which was nevertheless regarded as a considerable victory for the local opposition.

Part II
COLONIAL ALGERIA, 1870–1930

4
THE TRIUMPH OF THE SETTLERS, 1870–1930

Rebellions and Insurrection, 1870–71

The unexpected collapse of the Second Empire in the war with
Prussia (July 1870–January 1871) was greeted with joy by the
French of Algeria, who since 1863 had all been confirmed
republicans. 'Ever since Napoleon III uttered the words "Arab
Kingdom" we have been republicans, relentless enemies of
the Empire.' The most active called themselves democrats, saying that the will of the people (in other words their own will)
should prevail. They meant to destroy the military regime and
get on with colonisation without having to take the Muslims into
account.

The weeks that followed the surrender of the Emperor at
Sedan on 2 September saw the appearance at Algiers of a *comité
de défense*, formed from the political clubs that sprang up for
democracy and headed by the lawyer Vuillermoz, who had been
exiled to Algeria for his part in the Revolution of 1848. Under
his leadership it aspired to purge the administration and rule
the country in concert with other such committees in other
towns in Algeria. Having obtained from the Government of
National Defence, which was carrying on the war from Tours
and Bordeaux, a series of decrees to bring in the civil regime
they wanted, these committees procured the recall of the senior
administrators, the prefects of the *départements* and the acting
governor General Durrieu, and went on to demand a civil
governor. Algiers rejected the first nominee, another general,
who was forcibly expelled from the country by the militia and
the mob which invaded the *hôtel du gouvernement* (government

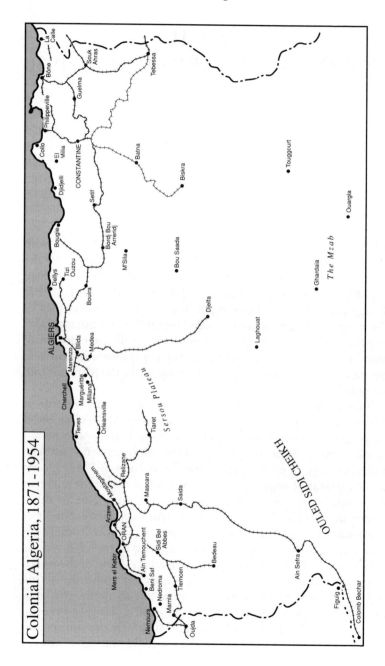

Colonial Algeria, 1871-1954

house) on 28 October. The deputy he left in charge could not take up his post, and remained a refugee in the Admiralty on its small island in the harbour. The committees felt free to take the destiny of Algeria into their own hands. 'Algeria *farà da se*', telegraphed Vuillermoz on 7 November, and the committee of Constantine concurred: 'We are going to make sure of our independence at last.'

However, when the government in France announced its intention of crushing 'the rebellion', Algiers accepted General Lallemand as commander of the army, and a journalist from Oran, Du Bouzet, as Commissioner of the Republic to take charge of the administration. Suddenly, the Algerian separatist movement died; the government which was to have been born from the Federation of Defence Committees never saw the light of day. Nevertheless, the dream of home rule for Algeria had been glimpsed, and meanwhile in Algiers the new Commissioner was unable, despite the proclamation of a state of emergency on 1 February 1871, to exercise his authority in the face of renewed rioting. The municipal elections on 5 February produced a vote of no confidence in his administration, and Du Bouzet was dismissed.

The revolutionary *commune* of Algiers was having its way with his feeble successor when the insurrection of the Muslim population spread across the country. The Europeans in the towns were stupefied, having discounted what they called 'the theory of revolts'. 'Four men and a corporal will be enough,' declared Vuillermoz as the tribes entered into rebellion. But Thiers, the old and determined statesman who had become head of the newly-elected French government with a mandate to restore law and order, sent troops and a strong man, Admiral de Gueydon, to take matters in hand. Algiers, which was to have been the 'Cadiz of the Revolution' (a reference to the rising which had driven the monarchy from Spain in 1868), gave way with a bad grace. The *commune* of Algiers was no more.

The Algerian insurrection of 1871, on the other hand, was quite another matter, even if it did not loosen the French hold on the country. It had its roots in the piled-up discontent of the Muslim population, the installation of the civil regime, the disasters of the war of 1870, and finally in the desire of the native

Algerians to recover their independence. Well before 1870, their chiefs had watched their influence being whittled away by the French authorities with growing irritation. At the same time relations between Europeans and Muslims had soured to the point of alarming those in charge. The announcement of the civil regime on 9 March 1870 provoked widespread resignations of their commands by the chiefs and the first unrest among the tribes. The departure of French troops and their subsequent defeat gave the conquered an unexpected opportunity to turn the tables. Fear of the new regime and the hope of expelling the foreign master explain the rush to arms by rather more than a third of the population.

For Muslims the introduction of the civil regime spelt 'settler rule': the confiscation of their lands, government by European mayors, the loss of their own civil laws and justice dispensed by juries of *colons*, all of which they dreaded. The Algerian press, with eighteen political newspapers in 1870, had served to warn the Arab chiefs that they stood to lose their posts and their privileges, and would be excluded from the *conseils généraux*, the Departmental assemblies. The *cadis* knew that they would be ousted from their courts by French justices of the peace. The first measures of the Government of National Defence when it took over from Napoleon III only confirmed their misgivings. Inspired by delegates from Algeria and partly drafted by a member of the *conseil général* of Constantine, one Viguier, successive enactments brought trial by jury into the assizes, the naturalisation of native Algerian Jews, and the extension of territory under civilian administration. The application of the *sénatus-consulte* of 1863 controlling the ownership and sale of land was suspended, and the *conseils généraux* as constituted under the Empire were dissolved.

The disappearance from the scene of Napoleon III and all the generals and officers who had won the friendship of the Arab chiefs, the absence of an energetic civilian governor who might have sought to reassure them, drove the *djouad*, the military aristocracy, to despair. A show of arms appeared the only honourable course; by demonstrating their power, they hoped still to show that they were indispensable. That was the calculation of most of the lords of the Constantinois, in particular a *bachagha* of the Medjana, a fiercely proud noble, Mohammed el Mokrani. The rural masses of the *bled* (the countryside) reacted more spontaneously to the news of the French defeats. The 'Sultan of the French', Napoleon III, was a prisoner and France no longer had a chief; a Jew — Crémieux, Minister of Justice at Tours — was in charge. With Paris conquered, the 'French tribes' were going to abandon it, and France would break up. A letter from Mahieddin, the son of Abd el-Kader, which was read out in the *djemaas* or native assemblies, called for insurrection. The *hadar* or Muslims of the cities, who were the most hostile of all to the French, took sharp note of the prevailing anarchy, of the way in which army officers returning from the war were attacked as 'surrenderers', and of the anti-clerical demonstrations. Some of them appealed to England for protection, as they had at the time of the conquest. Muslims in general thought that the French had gone mad, that the judgement of God had overtaken them, and that the hour of deliverance had come.

While the chiefs, all jealous of each other, reactivated the traditional *coffs* or tribal factions, new 'leagues of peasants and proletarians' appeared. Quite spontaneously, new rebel *djemaas* and *chartyas* (Ar. *shartiyya*), 'committees of public safety' or war councils were elected to control the *caids*, impose fines, seize the goods of those who would not join the common cause, and buy horses, arms and ammunition. In the region of El Milia one tribe took the initiative and fought entirely by itself. The *spahis* of the *smalas*, native auxiliaries organised in camps, refused at the end of January 1871 to embark for France. Rebels and mutineers besieged Souk-Ahras. Matters came to a head when Mokrani, who out of spite or resentment had let such preparations go forward right in his own fief, unleashed the revolt of the warrior nobles. Despite the ending of the Franco-Prussian war in January, and the certainty of seeing French troops arrive the following month, Mokrani and his brothers declared war on 14 March 1871. But their league of lords partly collapsed, and Mokrani was obliged to appeal to his opponents, the plebeian, egalitarian and religious Kabyles, under the leadership of the Rahmāniyya brotherhood. The old *shaykh* of the brotherhood, El Haddad, and more particularly his politically-minded son Si Aziz accepted the alliance with the Ouled Mokran, the Mokrani clan, and proclaimed the holy war on 8 April 1871.

In response to the call, the *moqaddems* and the *khouan*,[1] the priors and brothers of the order, launched the mass rising of the tribes of Greater and Lesser Kabylia. Those of the Hodna, of the western Sahara and the Beni Menacer rose up one by one under other chiefs. In all, some 800,000 people joined the rebellion. In the region of Algiers the majority of tribes, restrained by their chiefs, did not budge. Nor did they in the Oranais, where the people of the Tell were under the surveillance of regular troops, and moreover feared the *razzias* of the Ouled Sidi Cheikh Cheraga, who had been in rebellion since 1864.

There was in fact no coordination among the 100,000 or so *mujāhidin* or holy warriors, who without proper arms were unable to make any significant progress in the face of the French columns. Nevertheless, the struggle lasted seven months. The chiefs of the Raḥmāniyya were the first to lay down their arms, on 30 June, but the Kabyles of the Babors mountains continued the fight until September. El Mokrani, as soon as he knew of the presence in Algiers of 'a man of breeding', the governor de Gueydon, made offers of submission. The governor did not reply. El Mokrani was killed in the fighting and replaced by his brother Bou Mezrag, who continued the hopeless combat until he died of exhaustion in the desert on 20 January 1872.

The subsequent repression was intended to terrorise the natives into submission once and for all — also to procure lands and money for colonisation. The rebels were made to pay indemnities to the value of 35 million francs; in addition, their lands were sequestrated and much of it was confiscated. Seven tribal groups had their territory annexed to the state domain, a total of 309,614 ha., of which 73,000 ha. were later restored; 306 others had to give up 240,000 ha. and pay 8,926,000 francs to recover the remainder. But since such a sum was far beyond the means of the tribes concerned to pay in cash, it could only be found by selling a substantial portion of the lands in question back to the state at the fixed price of 50 francs a hectare for cultivated land and 10 francs a hectare for pasture. In this way not only were 446,000 ha. actually confiscated, but a further sum of 10,881,443 francs was obtained. Of this amount more than half was accounted for by yet more land surrendered for colonisation, especially in the Oranais. For the rebel population

[1] Arabic *ikhwān*, 'brothers', the followers of a *ṭarīqa*.

as a whole, the total cost of the war thus came to almost 65 million francs, or 70.4 per cent of the capital of those affected. Some tribes needed twenty years to repay their debts. For the majority, it meant ruin.

The native population, not only defeated but despoiled, never forgave what had been done, but there were no more great armed revolts. The rising of El Amri in 1876 affected only one tribe, and the disturbances in the Aures in 1879 two. The so-called rebellion of the southern Oranais in 1881 was more of a Saharan *razzia* in the context of the turbulent tale of the Ouled Sidi Cheikh. It was in fact the failure of the dissidents stirred up by Bou Amama, 'the Man with a Turban', that allowed 'a businesslike peace' to be concluded with the Ouled Sidi Cheikh. A more unexpected consequence was the annexation of the Mzab, the Saharan oases of the Ibadi sect, 'an enclave subject [since 1853] to a regime of limitless freedom, setting the worst kind of example to its neighbours'.

Algeria Assimilated to France, 1871–96

The defeat of the rebels of 1871 ensured the political victory of the *colons*. The French military, who were held to be either responsible for the insurrection or accomplices of the rebels, were discredited. So too was any kind of protectorate tending to favour the advancement of the Muslims. The French of Algeria henceforth imposed their will almost without opposition. Algeria became 'a small French Republic' in which only the interests of the French settlers counted. The voter's card became the title of nobility in this novel feudal system.

Admiral de Gueydon, governor in 1871–3, largely shared the views of the *colons*. His intention was 'not to perpetuate the national identity of the natives', but rather 'to break down the resistance of Arab society' by abolishing the native chieftaincy. He extended the zone of civil administration to 31,520 square km. and prepared a special code of law for the native population, the so-called *indigénat*.[2] However, he did refuse to

---

[2] The *Code de l'indigénat*, when finally enacted in 1881, gave the administration the power to fine or imprison the natives, individually and collectively, without trial for various offences supposedly subversive of law and order.

entrust the government of all natives to French mayors, but created instead huge *circonscriptions cantonales* or administrative districts in the care of civil or military commissioners. His successor General Chanzy (1873–9), a former officer of the *bureaux arabes*, likewise pursued the policy of assimilation and colonisation, creating for example 126 new settler villages. But he also tried to moderate the demands of the civilians and to rely once again upon the military and the Muslims. Finally, under pressure from his entourage, he abandoned the attempt, but not without arousing the opposition of the *colons* and their elected representatives, who eventually procured his recall. He had in fact accepted the further extension of the civil territory to 48,650 square km, as well as the multiplication of the *communes de plein exercice*, of which there were ninety-six in 1869 and 176 in 1879. Against the wishes of the *colons*, however, he succeeded in generalising the category of *circonscriptions cantonales* created by his predecessor under the old name of *communes mixtes*, mixed communes, which they retained.

His successor Albert Grévy (1879–1881), 'the first civil governor who really was a civilian' as well as a republican, undertook to give the Republicans of Algeria full satisfaction by suppressing the greater part of the military administration. With one stroke of the pen he placed the whole of the Tell — the most fertile and densely settled area of the country — under the authority of an improvised body of European administrators and mayors; the territories left under military rule had no more than 500,000 inhabitants. At the end of 1881 the civil territories, now covering 104,830 square km, were re-divided into 196 *communes de plein exercice* and seventy-seven *communes mixtes*. The *communes de plein exercice*, which were supposed to be fully equivalent to those in metropolitan France, actually bore very little resemblance to them. In 1879 one-third had an area of more than 10,000 ha., and some more than 30,000. Arab *douars* — very often whole tribes — had in fact been attached to these communes so as to supply them with most of their budget. When the *communes de plein exercice* increased in number, from 209 in 1884 to 261 in 1900, their size decreased but the spoiling of the *douars* continued; according to the local expression, the communes lived 'by eating *indigène*'. 'As far as the native is concerned', wrote Jules Ferry, 'the *commune de plein exercice* is daylight robbery.' Left without any supervision by the administration, the French mayors arranged the budget solely for the benefit of the Europeans while taxing the natives as they pleased.

The *communes mixtes* which succeeded the *circonscriptions cantonales* were even larger, with an average of 113,000 ha. and 20,000 inhabitants, almost all Muslim. They were in the hands of 'civilians in epaulettes' or uniformed administrators in civil territory, to which the great majority belonged. Compared to the seventy-three under civilian administration in 1900, a mere six were under military rule in military territory. In principle, the *communes mixtes* were intended to evolve into *communes de plein exercice*; fortunately for the Muslims, this development was very slow. The last category — *communes indigènes* (native communes), of which there were twelve in 1900 — applied only to the most isolated military territories where there were no Europeans at all. The arrival of a minimum of settlers or other European civilians turned them into *communes mixtes*.

In the name of assimilation, Algeria welcomed all French laws in the fields of political representation and justice. Invoking the special interests of the colony, it resisted French direct taxation and military service, introduced in November 1875 but reduced to one year only for French Algerians. Algeria likewise contrived to keep half the *impôts arabes*, the Arab taxes, for the *conseils généraux* of the *départements*, in which the Muslims were no longer represented except by six assessors nominated in accordance with one of Crèmieux' decrees. The Europeans had tried to get rid of even these, 'because their presence was an affront to the dignity of French citizens', but Chanzy had refused. The same campaign was waged against Muslim municipal councillors, who comprised at most one-third of the municipal body. On 7 April 1884 the Algerian members of parliament won a decree by which a very small, highly restricted number of native electors would be able to choose no more than six municipal councillors, and then only if they did not exceed a quarter of the total council. Such Muslim councillors, moreover, might no longer participate in the election of mayors and deputy mayors.

The policy of administrative assimilation received further encouragement with the *système de rattachements* or direct administration by the various ministries in Paris, which was devised by Algerian deputies and introduced in 1881. With Algeria integrated into France, all Algerian affairs were to be regulated from the capital, while the powers of the governor were reduced to the point at which he was nothing more 'than an inspector of colonisation in the palace of a nominal king'. The Algerian members of parliament, whose numbers were now double what they had been, were henceforth the only people to deal with Parisian civil servants ignorant of Algerian realities. Deputies as influential as Thomson or Eugène Etienne became the real masters of Algeria under a governor as nondescript as Tirman (1881–91). They were to remain so despite a lively metropolitan reaction against the administrative and political practices of settler Algeria.

In 1891, in a conscientious report, the deputy Burdeau highlighted the faults of the policy of *francisation* or 'Frenchification', the chosen weapon of the *colons* against the Muslims. The following year Jonnart, former director of the *Service de l'Algérie*, the Algerian section of the Ministry of the Interior, set out the realities of the Algerian administration in a report which became famous. The Senate or Upper Chamber, exasperated by the disclosure of yet more scandals, obtained the resignation of Governor Tirman, and set out to conduct a grand inquiry into Algerian affairs. The Commission of Enquiry of Eighteen (senators) under the former prime minister Jules Ferry, collected the statements of numerous witnesses and concluded almost unanimously with a condemnation of the methods in use in the colony. Ferry sharply criticised the misdeeds of administrative assimilation, the policy of *refoulement* or 'pushing back' the Arabs, the sequestration of their lands, the harshness of the forestry regime, and the greed and racial discrimination displayed by the part of the French community. He condemned 'the attitude of the *colon* to the conquered; it is difficult to make the European settler understand that there are other rights than his own in an Arab country', and that 'the native is not for exploitation at will'. Hence the programme of reform which he put to his colleagues in the Commission and which is summed up entirely in the words: 'We must not sacrifice the interests of the native population to the European element in any way.' In short, he demanded that France once again take up its role of árbitrator in this country 'inevitably given over to the conflict of two rival races', and that the governor-general should be given the power to counter-balance the weight of colonisation.

These proposals were speedily put to the test. Nominated on the recommendation of Jules Ferry in place of the candidates put forward by the Algerian interest, a governor of great distinction, Jules Cambon (1891–7), was the public enemy in Algeria from the day of his appointment onwards. This resolute and far-sighted politician, who was not going to sacrifice the Muslims but was determined to implement Ferry's reform programme was relentlessly opposed by the *élus* or elected representatives of the *colons* both in Algeria and in Paris. Applauded rather than supported by Parliament, he saw almost all his projects blocked by the Ministry of the Interior or in committee by the Algerian lobby. Even though he finally obtained, on 31 December 1896, the abolition of *rattachements* and an increase in the powers of the governor-general, he was almost immediately 'relieved of his office at the repeated insistence of Thomson and Etienne'. His dismissal demonstrated that in normal circumstances no policy of metropolitan origin could succeed any longer. France could no longer insist on its point of view except in times of emergency, a serious crisis, a war or a native insurrection. Algeria 'assimilated to France' was in fact in the hands of its colonial inhabitants.

The Development of Colonisation, 1870–1930

Reacting against the policy of Napoleon III, republican Algeria committed itself to official colonisation, hoping to bring about French settlement in rural areas thanks to free grants of land conditional upon obligatory residence. The first to be chosen were the émigrés from Alsace-Lorraine, who had fled into France when these provinces were annexed by Germany following the Franco-Prussian war. When the terms of the peace treaty were approved on 1 March 1871, they were promised 100,000 ha. of good land; but since they were mostly factory workers, their emigration to Algeria was a failure. Of the 1,183 families who were settled there at the huge cost of 6,500 frs. per family, only 387 remained on the land. Official colonisation then gave preference to the peasants of south-eastern France, or to the Algerian French themselves. This proved more successful, and in ten years 4,000 families had arrived from France. Between 1871 and 1882 a total of 347,268 ha. worth 43 million frs. was provided free for settlement, while the administration created a further 197 settler villages with 30,000 inhabitants, almost half of whom, 14,137 to be precise, had been recruited in the country. But the condition of obligatory residence was easily circumvented, and many of the concessionaires farmed their land with native sharecroppers. Many others resold their allocations, and by 1882, 2,331 families had given up what they had received.

Thus, to establish 'our domination in the Tell, a new wave of immigration' seemed necessary. The Algerian deputies pretended that the costs of settlement had not risen above 16,500,000 frs., and in 1881 they asked France for 50 million to set up 175 villages on 380,000 ha. of land. Since 300,000 ha. were to be 'obtained' from the natives, this meant a vast new campaign of expropriation. Supported as it was by the republicans, the proposal was attacked by all liberals, led by the Société française pour la protection des indigènes, and was rejected. Official colonisation thereafter slowed down but it did not cease, since land was made available from the state domain by a certain amount of expropriation and by purchase. So from 1881 to 1890, 3,206 plots totalling 176,000 ha. were granted, the majority freely, although some farms were sold at auction to proprietors who then leased their lands to Muslims. After 1887, the operation to establish the rights of the state to land in Algeria, begun by the *sénatus-consulte* of 1863, was resumed under the so-called new or 'little' *sénatus-consulte*. Applied until 1899 to 224 tribes that had escaped the original decree, it allocated without cost a further 957,000 ha. to the state domain, quite apart from the lands awarded to the *communes*. As a result, a further 120,097 ha. were handed over to the Europeans between 1891 and 1900, bringing the total for the years 1871–1900 to approximately 687,000 ha.

Private colonisation made similar strides. It was facilitated in the first place by the law of 1873, the so-called 'settlers' law' to which the veteran campaigner Dr Warnier gave his name, and subsequently by the 'little *sénatus-consulte*' of 1887, designed to replace Napoleon's statute. Under the pretext of abolishing allegedly collective property, the Warnier law aimed to break up undivided tribal property and enable the plots of the joint owners to be alienated. With the complicity of lawyers and estate agents, various interpretations and procedures, more shrewd than legal, increased the effectiveness of the law even more. The legal approval of the sale of an entire property belonging jointly to its owners under the Islamic law of *melk* (freehold), in order to provide the speculative European purchaser of one tiny share with its exact value, would bring about the ruin of the community and the acquisition by the European of vast estates at little cost. Until 1890 the administration turned a blind eye to such scandals, and only when they were revealed to parliament did the Warnier law cease to be applied. On the other hand the administration defended to the utmost, right up till 1922, *arch* or tribal property held in common under customary law (as distinct from Islamic law), which was declared to be inalienable. Colonisation therefore continued its campaign for an end to the administrative guardianship of these lands, and their 'complete *francisation*'. As time went on, the continual interpretation and amendment of the whole corpus of land legislation made it increasingly complex, to the point at which it placed its own restrictions upon private colonisation. Nevertheless, from 1880 to 1908 the private purchase of land in Algeria resulted in the net acquisition by the *colons* of 450,823 ha. From all sources, French colonisation thus succeeded in obtaining, in the space of less than thirty years (roughly from 1871 to 1898), at least a million hectares, more than twice as much as the 481,000 it had gained between 1830 and 1870.

By comparison, the expansion of the European rural population was much less rapid, rising from 119,000 in 1871 to about 200,000 in 1900. Although most of these *colons* were still French, an influx of Spanish and Maltese agricultural labourers quickly came to reinforce and then replace them. The Republic seemed nevertheless to have succeeded in its gamble: a class of European peasants was implanted in Algeria, representing more than a third of the total European population. Moreover, the French among them were not the beggars of popular myth.

Most were proprietors or well-to-do leaseholders, who had come to seek their fortune. Individual cases apart, the land of Algeria was less a frontier for the pioneer than an opportunity for the investor or speculator. The *colons* never entirely rooted themselves in it; for them agriculture was more a business than a way of life.

Up until 1880, wheat remained the staple of colonisation. Only its cultivation allowed the small settler without capital to become established. However, with the growth of money-lending shops giving farmers credit at a discount, and following the world fall in cereal prices, the *colons* tried a particularly speculative crop, the vine. The ruin of the French vineyards by phylloxera gave them their opportunity. Thanks to the generous provision of credit, the Tell was soon covered in vines, the area of European vineyards rising from 15,000 ha. in 1878 to 110,000 in 1890. Some centres of colonisation, some towns which had previously stagnated, made their fortune out of wine.

Crises arising from price falls, market failures or the scarcity of credit did not stop this rapid development, which by 1903 had reached 167,000 ha., and went on to its triumphant peak in the years 1907–14. In those same years, moreover, wheat became once again a speculative crop thanks to the North American technique of dry-farming. Developed to make the commercial production of cereals possible in regions of low rain-fall, this called for a three-year cycle of fallow, ploughing and sowing over a very wide area, only possible on large farms. Thanks to dry-farming, the fields of European cereals spread far to the south, beyond the Mediterranean climate of the Tell across the high plains of the Sersou plateau in the west and the Constantinois in the east. Such prosperity, so long in coming, permitted a new leap forward.

The 'oil-stain' of colonisation continued to spread in the golden age of the years before 1914. Huge purchases of land by the newly-rich settlers, amounting to 427,000 ha. between 1909 and 1917, were coupled with the resumption of official colonisation and the granting away of more than 200,000 ha. between 1901 and 1914, of which 53,000 were free, to bring the total of farm land at the disposal of the Europeans to 2,123,288 ha. in 1917, plus 194,159 ha. of forest. After large sales of at least 113,306 ha. in the post-war years 1918–21, which gave rise briefly to thoughts of a serious crisis, these figures were soon on the increase again. In 1930, approximately 2,350,000 ha. belonged to the *colons*, rising to 2,462,537 ha. in 1934. Out of this total in 1930, 1,468,677 ha. had been provided through official colonisation; the remainder had come from the purchase of some 1,712,000 ha. for the sum of 562 million frs. The final figure was accounted for by the resale to Muslim Algerians of about 700,000 ha. for 530 million frs. Meanwhile, from 1928 onwards new legislation at long last facilitated the subjection of *arch* or tribal territory to the French law of private property, opening up for liquidation a category of land that had been largely beyond the reach of the market.

However, the rural European population had ceased to grow. From 1906 to 1926 it remained almost static, passing from 34.6 per cent of the total European population to 28.6 per cent. This relative decline, together with the beginning of an absolute fall in numbers, was symbolically acknowledged in 1930, when France finally abandoned the policy of official agricultural colonisation. What had in fact been happening from a very early date was the amalgamation of small properties, little farms which were economically doomed in a country geographically favourable to *latifundia* or great estates, and now given over to speculative crops for the export market. In the process, the settlers themselves had been squeezed out. Since before 1914, no more than 40 per cent of the European agricultural population were landowners while 20 per cent rented their farms, turning two-fifths into wage-earners, a proportion that by 1930 had crept up to 43 per cent.

The huge estates then common throughout the country, with a quarter of European landowners in possession of farms larger than 100 ha., had put an end to agricultural immigration from rural France. The vine, which was to have created in Algeria a population of small wine-producers as in France, at first merely prolonged the survival of the cereal-growers introduced by official colonisation. Subsequently the great grain or vine-growing properties absorbed their concessions and spat out the people. In the Sersou, the settlements plots of 50–70 ha. gave way to estates of 4–5,000 ha. Developments like this meant that in 1930 there were actually only 26,153 European

properties, between them covering 2,345,667 ha. Moreover, a
fifth of these had an average of 318 ha. each, and by themselves
accounted for 1,721,979 ha. or 74 per cent of the whole; 18 per
cent fell between 50 and 100 ha. amounting to 364,366 ha. in
all. The rest were mere parcels. In other words, already in 1930
colonisation was no more than a commercial venture on the part
of a class of European businessmen; this was the very destiny
which the hated experts of the Second Empire had prescribed
for it. Given over to cash crops for wholesale export, to the point
at which 50 per cent of the country's export earnings came from
wine and its related products, agricultural colonisation enriched
European Algeria but lost all colonial justification. It restricted
the growth of the French population while competing in the
market with metropolitan producers. Algerians themselves criticised it for sacrificing food-crops and condemning the country
to the risks of monoculture.

Urban settlement developed alongside rural colonisation, but
always involved much greater numbers. The European towns,
first administrative and then economic centres, attracted —
in addition to French civil servants and tradespeople — foreigners of all nationalities; there were no less than 260,000
immigrants from Europe between 1870 and 1900. While 60 per
cent of Europeans in 1860 were town-dwellers, this proportion
increased to 63.2 per cent in 1886, 65.4 per cent in 1906 and
71.4 per cent in 1926. The towns, especially the small ones,
became the real Algerian melting-pot. As a result, in spite of
official colonisation and the naturalisation of the Jews, the
foreigners always seemed likely to outnumber the French. The
law of 26 June 1889 therefore granted French citizenship to all
children of foreigners who did not expressly refuse it; naturalisation became automatic. In this way a numerical preponder-
ance of French nationals was assured. In 1886 there were
219,000 French as against 211,000 foreigners; ten years later
the figures were 318,000 French, of whom 50,000 were naturalised, against 212,000 foreigners; while in 1901, the French
numbered 364,000, including 72,000 naturalised, and the
foreigners only 189,000. The 'foreign peril', denounced by local
politicians for electoral purposes, was in fact less historically
important than the progressive fusion of the French with the
naturalised 'neo-French', resulting in the Algerianisation of

both. The total European population grew from 280,000 in 1872 to 578,000 in 1896, after which the number of Europeans / born in Algeria rose above the number of immigrants. A new people was coming into existence, which prompted certain politicians and some agitators to think that the time for a 'free Algeria' had arrived.

An Abortive Revolution, 1898–1900

What was commonly known as the 'anti-Jewish crisis' may have been set off by the notorious Dreyfus affair in France, but it was in fact an abortive Algerian revolution. There were indeed some anti-Jewish riots, but hostility to the Metropole and the dream of an independent Algeria were the principal motives, which explain the seriousness of what happened.

Anti-Jewish prejudice had always been strong in the colonial population, especially among the lower classes of Spanish descent. These people were deliberately roused by radical politicians who reckoned that they were being kept out of power by the Algerian Jews, who voted collectively according to the directives of their consistories or community organisations and were allegedly manipulated by electoral agents. The socialists, inspired by their anti-capitalism, showed themselves as ferociously anti-Semitic as the extreme right; on the orders of the demagogue Drumont, newly arrived from France, they raged against the system. An 'Algerian' student, Massimiliano Milano, called Max Régis, put himself at the head of anti-Semites and autonomists alike, and announced in January 1898 'the hour of the Revolution': 'We will water the tree of our liberty with Jewish blood.'

From 20 to 25 January the Algiers mob ruled the streets, and colonial Algeria approved; in May 1898 four 'anti-Jewish' deputies were elected to the National Assembly. But the anti-Jewish front broke up when the Milano brothers tried to appeal to the foreigners in the European population against France, and when the governor, Laferrière, announced concessions from Paris to the colony's 'need for autonomy'. On 25 August 1898 Algeria received not only the coveted promise of financial independence, but also the immediate creation of an elected colonial assembly, the *délégations financières*. At the same time the *conseil supérieur de l'Algérie*, the nominated body which advised the governor, was reorganised and reinforced by elected members. The latter now became the majority in this controlling instrument of the administration.

The law of 29 December 1900 conferred on Algeria its own civil status and provided for a special budget. Claims for autonomy were satisfied; the wine-based economy made it impossible for the *colons* seriously to demand an end to the customs union with France. Algerian protest subsided and the movement for independence, now reduced to the hard core of 'anti-Semites', foundered in excited words, demonstrations and revolutionary-style disorders by so-called 'anti-Semitic nationalist youth', which led in Algiers to the sack of the *Maison du Peuple* and the setting-up of a fortified redoubt, the *Bon Accueil* ('warm welcome') as a headquarters for the militants. A minor incident rapidly restored calm: on 26 April 1901 the colonial village of Margueritte was attacked by about a hundred natives. The denunciation of 'the native peril' which this provoked reminded everyone of the existence of the Arab-Berber population.

5

THE PROGRESS OF
ALGERIAN MUSLIMS AND THE
'NATIVE POLICY', 1870–1930

The Development of Muslim Society

Muslim society did not resist the progress of colonisation; with
its framework broken, it collapsed. The decline of the great
families, which had begun under the Second Empire, accelerated after 1870. Always under suspicion and excluded from
positions of command and from office, they vegetated as their
poverty increased. Under constant attack and unable to adapt,
the traditional aristocracy seems to have disappeared completely by 1900. The *'grands chefs'* were never replaced, and the
only survivors were certain maraboutic families or patriarchal
dynasties in the south. The tiny traditional bourgeoisie in the
cities, composed of the literate, the learned and the merchant,
likewise vanished with the shock of colonialism, and re-emerged
only very slowly in the early 1900s, and then in a different
form. Native craftsmanship was simply blown to pieces, and
survived only in traditionalist cities like Tlemcen and Constantine. Otherwise only domestic handicrafts remained. As for the
Arab peasantry, victims of continual dispossession which was
made all the worse by sales of lands forced upon the ruined
fellah, they were hit equally hard.[1] The impoverishment which
was so apparent to contemporaries has been denied, but recent
studies have shown that it was far more widespread than
was ever suspected. Rediscovered and renamed *'clochardisation'*
(beggaring), the phenomenon went back at least as far as 1870.

---

[1] According to the agricultural statistics, the area of land privately owned
by *indigènes* in civil territory decreased from 8,188,140 ha. in 1883 to
5,791,255 ha. in 1903, a fall of 29 per cent in twenty years. The enquiry of
1900, however, reckoned that there were 7,281,838 ha. of such property
coupled with 1,912,000 ha. of *arch* land, while that of 1917 gave 6,460,034 ha.
of privately-owned land to the Muslims in Algeria north of the Sahara, and
2,766,934 ha. of *arch* land.

It was long fashionable to attribute such alterations in peasant society, notably the sedentarisation of nomads and semi-nomads, to the workings of so-called progressive policies, when in truth such settlement was spontaneous, having been provoked by general economic change and the squeezing to death of the tribes.

Since the Arab peasantry practised a low-yielding, extensive form of agriculture which left the land fallow for periods of two years, it was particularly sensitive to the shrinkage of the cultivable area at its disposal. In the same way, the advance of colonisation, the closing of forest pasture and the raising of rents for nomadic grazing land led to a decline in livestock and in nomadism. Algeria, 'land of sheep', had 8 million in 1865, 7.7 million in 1885 and 6.3 million in 1900. But if one takes account of population growth, each Arab — statistically speaking — had three sheep in 1887 and only one and a half in 1900. The corresponding figures for native-owned cattle were 1 million in 1867, 1,071,000 in 1887, and 846,000 in 1900, so that where in 1867 five Arabs owned between them almost two head of cattle, in 1900 they had only one. It is obvious why one cannot easily speak of progress, especially when the figures for Muslim cereal production tell a similar story. This was in any case very variable, linked to the vagaries of a notoriously unpredictable climate; but by comparison with the Europeans' production, it was in constant decline. In 1860 the Muslim harvest accounted for 80 per cent of the wheat produced in Algeria, in 1900 for 72 per cent and in 1938 for a mere 44 per cent. The area under native grown cereals, essentially hard wheat and barley with only a little soft wheat, was static or slightly reduced from 1873 to 1903, decreasing rapidly thereafter from 1906 to 1921, when it began to climb back towards its former level. But in spite of the multiplication of Arab ploughs, the number of which rose from one to every 85 ha. in 1865 to one to every 23 ha. in 1900, and the adoption of some French ploughs, the yields themselves declined, in the case of hard wheat, from an average of 4.1 quintals[2] per hectare to an average of 3.7 q. As cereals became restricted to poorer land, the area sown in the

---

[2] 1 quintal, abbreviation q., = 100 kilos or two hundredweight.

more fertile Tell retreated, while that of the dry steppe zone of the High Plains to the south expanded.

Meanwhile the Arab peasant, heavily burdened up till 1919 with a special and complicated tax regime, and without access to any agricultural credit, was not sheltered by his poverty from the vicissitudes of the European economy. Adversely affected by the long depression from 1873 to 1896, he should have benefited from the return of prosperity at the beginning of the twentieth century, but was unable to do so. The archaic marketing of grain and livestock, which were sold for low prices at harvest time and then bought back to bridge the gap before the next harvest, left him at the mercy of every passing slump, whose effects were aggravated by the practices of traditional usury. The colonial situation exacerbated rather than relieved a problem typical of a pre-modern agricultural economy, which was left all the more vulnerable to an even greater enemy than the market: the weather. Algeria continued to suffer as a result from famine, notably in 1893, 1897 and 1920, followed by deadly epidemics of cholera and typhus. Each surge of misery found its natural expression in an alarming wave of crime, although the administration was slow to admit the connection.

Muslim peasants took a long time to accept employment on European farms. Although they had always been ready to cultivate for the French as *khammes* or sharecroppers, they were much slower to work directly for the *colons*, who in any case preferred foreign, immigrant labour. The first native wage-earners were employed in the period of the Second Empire as harvesters, with sickles, and subsequently as seasonal workers or for particular jobs of work. Only after 1903 did they take the place of foreign workers as permanent farm labourers. But even in wine-growing areas, wage labour was less remunerative than the farming of their own little plots, or sharecropping, a fact which helps explain the late appearance of a wage-earning class and its secondary importance in the native economy. At the beginning of the twentieth century, those who owned their land or grazed their own animals represented, at 52 per cent, just over half the native peasantry. *Khammes* accounted for 30 per cent, farm labourers for 12 per cent, and those who rented their land for the remaining 5 per cent. These percentages gradually changed up till 1930; then, although the

proportion of proprietors and pastoralists remained at 52 per
cent of the Muslim agricultural population, the owners of
cultivated land represented only 24 per cent. The proportion
of agricultural wage-earners had gone up to 18 per cent and that
of *khammes* down to the same figure; renters were a mere 2 per
cent. However, overall statistics like these are still insufficient
to measure the true extent of peasant proletarianisation, and
those of landownership are little better for the purpose.

Around 1900, small-scale landowning by the native population appears to have predominated. In the Constantinois 55 per
cent of Arab owners had less than 10 ha., 20 per cent possessed
11–20 ha., and 12.4 per cent, 21–30 ha. Large estates were
statistically almost nonexistent, with only 0.8 per cent of landowners having more than 100 ha.; in any case they were
divided into small farms. However, they remained extremely
important socially. A landowning middle class was almost
unknown in the province. In the west, on the other hand, in
the valley of the Chelif, the great estates slipped from the hands
of the traditional aristocracy only to be reconstituted by a class
of *nouveaux riches*, while a rural middle class, 'perhaps 10 per
cent of the peasant world' of the region, came into existence
between the two world wars. Thus, in 1930, native landownership for the whole of Algeria was distributed as follows. A mere
1.13 per cent of proprietors possessed an average of 198 ha., but
alone accounted for 21 per cent of privately-owned land in
native possession. Similarly, 6 per cent owned an average of
43.1 ha., representing a further 21 per cent of land in native
ownership, while 23 per cent, with an average of 18.8 ha., took
up 35 per cent. On the other hand, no less than 70 per cent,
to a total of 434,537 individual owners, had on average no more
than 4 ha., or merely 23 per cent of the whole. In the absence
of comparable statistics from previous years, these figures point
to the existence, alongside the large landowners, of a small rural
middle class, perhaps of recent origin. At the same time,
however, they betray the impoverishment of the mass of small
landowners, too readily attributed to population growth alone.

Population pressure, weak at first but building up steadily,
remained moderate until 1930, although there is no doubt
that it caused the rural masses, whose means of subsistence
remained static, to become even poorer. The Muslim popula-

tion, which stood at 2,733,000 in 1861 and 3,577,000 in 1891, had grown to 4,923,000 in 1921. By 1930 it was thought to have doubled in seventy years, despite fluctuations during periods of economic crisis (1886–96) and war (1911–21). Up until then, urbanisation had been partial and slow, with only 6.9 per cent of Muslims living in towns in 1881, 7.6 per cent in 1906 and 10.8 per cent in 1931. Stimulated after the First World War by the overpopulation of the land in relation to available resources, the influx from the countryside affected both the small towns where workers were hired, and the big cities. It ensured that for the first time Europeans and Algerians began to live side by side in a big way, straining the relations between the two communities still further. At the same time it was the beginning of a rapid introduction of the Muslim population into the modern world. Emigration to France, which greatly speeded up the process, came into existence from 1910 onwards as a powerful weapon in the struggle against misery on the one hand and for self-improvement on the other. The war of 1914–18, followed by the suppression of travel permits in 1919, broadened the stream to 92,000 in 1923. The discovery of France and Europe by the Algerian *fellah* was a decisive turning-point in his history.

The 'Native Policy'

Even when the policy of assimilation was everywhere triumphant between 1870 and 1898, there was still no question of considering the Muslims as French. The very opposite was true: they were the victims of a policy of subjection. A special status, that of the *indigénat* or native population, was gradually introduced and progressively reinforced. In 1881 a *code de l'indigénat* or native penal code created a series of penalties unknown to common law for forty-one offences 'peculiar to the natives', scaled down to twenty-one in 1890. The purpose was to provide the administrative officers of the civil regime with the exceptional powers of the military to deal with tribes which were still not entirely submissive. But this 'provisional' authorisation to sentence without judgement and in practice without control, which was granted 'for seven years' to the administrators of the *communes mixtes*, was periodically renewed from 1881 to 1927. The same 'disciplinary powers' were entrusted in the *communes de plein exercice* to justices of the peace, who were able to condemn without right of appeal until 1914. The natives remained equally liable to special penalties of imprisonment, probation, collective fines, and individual or collective confiscations. A permit was required for all movement outside the *douar*, following the precedent established for black slaves in the French West Indies.

Where the policy of assimilation was employed, it was to wipe out the distinctive features of native society. In spite of the promises which had been made and partly kept until 1870, Muslim institutions were directly and indirectly attacked, especially between 1870 and 1890. After the gradual suppression of the great native chieftaincies, the target was Muslim justice. 'The Muslim judge must make way for the French judge', said Admiral de Gueydon; 'we are the conquerors, let us be so.' In 1874, judges of the peace, their powers enhanced, replaced the *cadis* in Kabylia. The Upper Council of Islamic Law was abolished in 1875, together with the consultative *medjles*, while the number of *mahakmas* or *cadis'* courts was progressively reduced from 184 to sixty-one in 1890. The war on the *cadis* culminated in the decree of 10 September 1886 which took away their competence to deal with all questions of real estate in the whole of Algeria. Henceforth the French justice of the peace was responsible for the application of both French and Muslim law. In criminal cases, Muslims were now to be judged in the assize courts by juries, all of whose members were chosen exclusively from the French population.

The instinctive pursuit of Frenchness changed the names of all towns and villages. For the same reason, the civil status introduced in 1882 seemed to Muslims a deliberate affront. Its frequent result was to provide Algerians with new patronymic surnames, of a kind hitherto unknown,[3] but which finally became the rule. Frenchness, however, did not go so far as to encourage a Christian policy of evangelisation; the various

[3] The typical pattern of Muslim names is simply 'Abd Allah son of Hasan son of Muhammad son of. . . . ; there is no constant surname equivalent to 'Muhammadsson'.

attempts on the part of the missionary order of White Fathers founded by the strongly evangelistic Mgr Lavigerie, archbishop of Algiers 1867–91, and Protestant missions, were blocked by the administration. They were perhaps rather too ready to take 'no' for an answer. Considering the extent to which Christians protested against the injustices of colonialism elsewhere in the world, it is curious how easily priests and missionaries accepted the colonial regime in Algeria.

In regard to Islam itself, the religious policy of the Third Republic was a mixture of wary toleration and a multiplicity of prohibitions. Although religious freedom was generally proclaimed, hardly any religious instruction was permitted. In the name of assimilation and subsequently secularisation, introduced into French education by the law of 1905 which separated Church from State, Koranic schools for children were strictly limited, and the schools of the *zaouias*, labelled 'Muslim monasteries', were kept under surveillance, harassed or closed. As a result, the class of *'ulamā'*, the doctors of the Islamic law, ceased to be recruited normally, and the number of *dherrar* and *mouderres*[4], primary Koranic teachers and professors, decreased. An unintended consequence was the decline in the knowledge of literary Arabic, which was scarcely taught. Religious observance was tightly controlled. If local festivals and pilgrimages were generally allowed to take place, subject to authorisation, the pilgrimage to Mecca was more rarely permitted, even though it was one of the five pillars of Islam; on various pretexts it was forbidden as an annual event so that departures could be spaced out. The French parliament had to intervene in 1913 to end these restrictions. Meanwhile, although Islam is a religion without priesthood or formal clergy, France took it upon itself to create and maintain an official Muslim clergy paid by the state and responsible for the conduct of worship in the mosques. For this reason the law which separated Church and State in France in 1905 was never applied to Islam in Algeria. The clergy themselves, trained in three French *medersas* or colleges, were to have countered the hold of the religious brotherhoods over the population. These brotherhoods, like the Qadiriyya and the Rahmaniyya, which had played a large part in the

---

[4] Arabic, *dharrār, mudarris*.

resistance to the French conquest, still enjoyed large follow-
ings, and were regarded with great suspicion by the authorities,
anxious to undermine any form of collective organisation on the
part of their Muslim subjects. However, it was quickly realised
that this 'clergy on oath' had little influence. Thus the administration preferred to rely on the leaders of the said brotherhoods
and upon the marabouts or local holy men. Compromised by
their collaboration, these in their turn gradually lost all their
prestige and authority.

In spite of the policy of assimilation and the French administrative tradition of standardisation, the Algerian administration discreetly practised a policy of divide and rule where the
natives were concerned. The Berbers of Algeria, speakers of
the various Berber languages but thought of in practice as the
mountain peoples of Greater and Lesser Kabylia, were considered more assimilable than others because, it was said, they
were only 'superficially islamised and hereditary enemies of the
Arabs'. Kabyle particularism, played up by a polemical literature, soon gave rise to a veritable Kabyle myth: the Kabyles
were held to be descendants of the Gauls(!), the Romans, Christian Berbers of the Roman period or the German Vandals(!).
Some therefore never lost the hope of 'giving them back their
Christian faith', which explains the attempts at conversion
made by Mgr Lavigerie between 1863 and 1870. They failed
completely. Nevertheless Kabylia, called 'the Auvergne of
Africa' from its alleged resemblance to the mountain peasant
country of the Massif Central in France, was supposed on the
one hand to receive French laws, and on the other to retain its
own customs. Thus Muslim judges were abolished or reduced
to the rank of notaries, Koranic schools were closed, and only
education in French schools was allowed. But in spite of some
curious attempts to speed up the introduction of French ways,
the major preoccupation was to defend the customary laws or
qanoun[5] against the Shari'a, the Islamic law, and to preserve
the region's own particular chiefs, the *amin*,[6] and its traditional tax system. The *djemaa* or village assemblies were sup-

---

[5] The term, lit. 'canon', derives from the name of the state code of non-
religious law in the Ottoman Empire.
[6] Arabic *amin*, pl. *umanā'*

pressed in law but tolerated in fact, and the use of Kabyle dialects was encouraged. In 1898 the Kabyles were given separate representation in the *délégations financières*, 'so that the two peoples of Algeria should not become used to contact with each other'. However, in practice this policy of divide and rule proved ineffective, for with the development of better communications, the Arabisation of the cantons of Kabylia went ahead, while the drive for Frenchness had separated out only a few individuals before the start of the great emigration of Kabyle workers to metropolitan France. The failure of the policy led to perpetual recriminations against the administration; down to the end of the colonial period it was accused, rightly or wrongly, 'of having Islamised and Arabised the Kabyle population'.

Other ways in which the rules of assimilation were bent were more deeply felt by the native populations, notably the way in which they were denied equality in terms of tax right up till 1919. As well as the *impôts arabes*, which were swollen by numerous little additions, Muslims had to pay the various direct French taxes that had been introduced into Algeria, not to speak of all the indirect ones. This double imposition lasted until 1919, when the *impôts arabes* were abolished; previously, in spite of continual demands by senior civil servants or members of parliament for their reform, the only changes deemed compatible with that famous respect for Muslim tradition were rises in the rate. Muslims who in 1870 paid 14 million frs. in *impôts arabes* and 22 million in all, paid on average 40,800,000 frs. per annum between 1885 and 1890, of which 19 million came from the *impôts arabes*. In spite of the growth in size of the population, the impoverishment of the Muslim community meant that these rates could not be sustained, and only returned to their former level between 1907 and 1914, when the total amounted to 45 million frs. in 1912. At the beginning of the twentieth century Muslim Algerians, who paid twice as many direct taxes as the Europeans, contributed 46 per cent of the taxes collected in Algeria for the various local and provincial budgets. Their average *per capita* payment, in the region of 10 frs., was certainly much less than the European average of 77 frs., but then the Muslims, according to an optimistic administrative estimate, possessed no more than 37 per cent of the wealth of Algeria, and their individual standard of living was vastly inferior. The examination of particular cases points to a thoroughgoing fiscal exploitation of the small native tax-payer, which is clearly illustrated by the figures following the reforms of 1919. The Muslim share of direct taxation then fell to 16 per cent, that of indirect taxation to 28 per cent, and that of the special budget for Algeria to 21 per cent, a dramatic reduction by almost half to 27 per cent of all budgets, special, departmental and communal.

Meanwhile a new native policy had been officially introduced from 1901 onwards, entitled the 'policy of association'. Rejecting the principle of legislative assimilation, this advocated 'the advancement of Muslims within their own civilisation'. This more generous approach did not, however, inspire any profound change in the attitude of the Algerian administration, which used it simply to justify yet more stretching of the rules of common law. Disregard went much further in 1902 in the wake of the attack upon the colonial village of Margueritte,[7] when special courts for Muslims only were set up by decree at the request of the *délégations financières*. Not only were special criminal courts introduced, but repressive tribunals were created to deal with threats to public order. The right of appeal was at first abolished, and even when it was restored was made very difficult. Governor-general Révoil, who brought in the measure, won great popularity among the *colons*, but was attacked by the radical left-wing leader Clemenceau, and dismissed as a result by the prime minister, Combes. Metropolitan opinion in general had shown itself almost unanimously opposed to the treatment of Muslims in Algeria when the Margueritte insurgents were brought before the assizes at Montpellier; eighty-one were acquitted and not one was condemned to death. In the general climate of opinion on both sides, the fact that the new criminal courts, unlike the *tribunaux répressifs*, were a long-considered attempt to put the principle of association into practice, was ignored.

Governor-general Jonnart, who had promised a reforming government in 1901, was now sent back in 1903 for what turned out to be a long tour of duty that lasted eight years. A former

[7] See above, p. 91.

Minister of Public Works, Jonnart concerned himself in particular with the economic infrastructure of Algeria. His efforts
were rewarded thanks above all to loans and to the boom of
the pre-war years, when the country's external trade almost
doubled from 666 million frs. in 1899 to 1,168 million in 1913.
But although he showed himself genuinely anxious to encourage
the progress of the Muslim population, he failed to gain acceptance for any of the proposed reforms to native policy and
administration. Only a decree of 1908 provided for the election
to the *conseils généraux* of six Muslim councillors by some 5,000
electors among whom were Muslim civil servants and *caïds*.
Social and medical assistance to Muslims remained more symbolic than real; there were only eighty 'native' infirmaries in
1910, and aid was given to 12,000 of the very poor. However,
even the benevolent intent of the policy was called in question
by Jonnart's successor Lutaud, an imperious administrator
who allied himself with the *colons* against the demands of parliament for reform.

France had hoped above all to conquer the minds of Algerians
through the schools. The Third Republic inherited a programme of schooling for the *indigène*, thirty-six primary Arab-
French schools with 1,300 Muslim pupils in 1870, two Arab-
French colleges and three *medersas*. But the republicans of
Algeria had the schools and colleges closed, and left the *medersas*
to stagnate; in 1882 only sixteen primary schools remained.
Jules Ferry, outraged by this 'ridiculous chauvinism', wanted
from 1880 onwards to create a network of fifteen government
schools, with three-quarters of the money coming from Paris.
In 1883 he applied to Algeria the legislation on education that
had recently been introduced in France; it provoked, he wrote,
'a general cry of indignation'. Appalled to find themselves liable
for the construction of schools for this crowd of beggars', the
French *communes* without exception turned down this 'costly
and dangerous experiment'. 'If education were widespread,
the unanimous cry of the native would be, Algeria for the
Arabs!' In 1890 only some 10,000 Muslim children, a mere 1.9
per cent of those of school age, attended public or private French
schools.

An admirably dedicated director of education, Jeanmaire,
struggled from 1884 to 1908 to develop the native schools

despite the obstinate prejudice of the settlers, who would accept
only practical vocational or agricultural training. By the time
when Jeanmaire was obliged to resign over his opposition to
the transformation of his 'native' into 'auxiliary' schools, the
so-called *écoles gourbis* or 'bush schools' introduced by the *délégations financières*, the number of Muslim children in receipt of
French primary education had risen to 33,397, or 4.3 per cent
of those of school age. That number had scarcely doubled by
1930, more than twenty years later. Despite the growth of the
auxiliary schools, which were entrusted to native instructors
instead of qualified French teachers, the percentage had
reached only 5 per cent in 1914, i.e. 47,263 pupils out of
850,000 children of school age. In 1929 there were 60,644
children in school out of some 900,000, roughly six per cent.
It is hardly surprising, then, that French secondary education
took in only about eighty-four pupils a year before 1900, and
150 before 1914. By then, the Faculty or University College of
Algiers had awarded Muslims a total of thirty-four *baccalauréats*
and twelve degrees.

For a long time Muslim parents were reluctant to send their
children, in particular their daughters, to the schools of 'the
beylik' or government. Indeed, it was often necessary to force
them to do so, especially since the leaders of the Muslim community were opposed to French education for fear of the consequences, namely the creation of an emancipated Europeanised
younger generation. Only after the First World War did young
Muslims themselves actually want to learn in French schools,
from which time education became one of the principal
demands of the so-called Muslim *évolués*, the Europeanised élite
who had 'evolved' out of traditional Muslim into French
civilisation, as they pressed for reform. By then a few Algerian
Muslims had taken their examinations in France, where after
1920 others came for their studies. But there were many more
who, from time immemorial, went to Fez, Tunis or Cairo for
a traditional Islamic education: the University of Al-Azhar in
Cairo had always more *tolba*[8] or students from Algeria than
the *medersa* of Algiers itself. Nevertheless the movement of
Muslim modernism, to bring Islam into the modern world,

[8] Arabic *tulabā'*, sing. *ṭālib*

came late to Algeria, and then essentially to the Constantinois. When the great Muslim reformer Muḥammad ʿAbduh came to Algeria from Egypt in 1903, he was struck by its conservative rigorism in matters of religion. Once again it was only after the First World War that the shaykh Ben Badis began his puritan preaching in 1924 in the name of Islamic reform, and opened the first 'revived' school in the name of a modern Islamic education.

The Political Advancement of the Muslim Population, 1900–1930

In the early years of the twentieth century a small secularised élite of Muslims from the cities, culturally French, put forward through its journals, discussion groups and associations the demands of the *évolués*. Opposed by the official Muslim establishment, the 'Old Turbans', and by the Algerian administration, these 'Young Algerians'[9] turned to metropolitan liberals such as Paul Bourde of *Le Temps* and Albin Rozet in parliament, and quickly gained the attention of enlightened French opinion. Their delegations to Paris explained their demands, which were above all political: with the aim of winning eventual political equality with the French of Algeria, they almost all urged the policy of assimilation, which for some of them had become an irrational, emotional ideal. Fearing an excess of metropolitan sentimentality, the Algerian government portrayed this demand for equality as a 'national movement against French occupation'. But these so-called 'nationalists' were in fact campaigning in favour of the compulsory conscription of Muslims proposed in parliament by Messimy. What they asked for in return was an end to fiscal inequality, the extension of primary education, an increase in the political representation of the Muslim population, and the abolition of the *'indigénat'* or native penal system.

The proposed military service alarmed not only the Europeans and the Old Turbans, who rejected it, but the pious

---

[9] The name echoed that of their contemporaries, the Young Tunisians and, more distantly, the Young Turks, although their action within the constitutional framework of French Algeria was very different.

citizens of Nedroma and Tlemcen, two hundred of whom followed the tradition of exile for the faith, and set out as *muhājirūn*[10] for Syria. The Exodus of Tlemcen in 1911 did not prevent the vote for the principle of native conscription, but it did lead to the claim for political compensations being intensified. In spite of the opposition of the Governor-general Lutaud, the government in Paris, faced with a Chamber and Senate in favour of a more liberal policy, was obliged to promise some amelioration of the legal and administrative condition of the native population. In 1914 internment for Muslims as an administrative measure was abolished, although marked individuals continued to be placed under surveillance, and disciplinary powers were generally reduced. The proposed political and administrative reforms were studied, but these were delayed by the First World War.

When war came in 1914, the loyalism of the natives came as a pleasant surprise to the government in Algeria. Only the isolated region of the Aurès in eastern Algeria rose up in 1916 against the compulsory call-up of men for military service, but the disturbances remained localised. Native recruitment provided 173,000 soldiers, of whom 87,500 were volunteers; 25,000 Muslim troops and, be it said, 22,000 French Algerians, died in battle. In addition, 119,000 Algerian workers went over to help the war effort; by 1918 more than a third of the male population of Algeria were being employed in France.

Such an effort seemed to Clemenceau to deserve a substantial political reward, but the announcement of his intentions provoked not only the agitation of the French in Algeria but the resignation of Lutaud. He thereupon sent back to Algiers the former governor-general, Jonnart, to negotiate the acceptance of his reforms. Taking *colon* opinion into account, Jonnart eliminated the most daring measures, notably those which, in accordance with the plans of the Second Empire, would have allowed the *élus* — the elected representatives of the Muslim community — to participate in the election of deputies and senators to the French Assembly. At least as far as parliament was concerned, there was then no problem.

---

[10] From *hijra*, which recalls the emigration of Muhammad from Mecca to Medina in 622.

Fiscal equality between Muslims and Europeans was brought about by the introduction of new taxes on the metropolitan model. The various laws and decrees of February-March 1919 enlarged the Muslim electorate for all the Algerian assemblies, bringing it to 100,000 for the *conseils généraux* and *délégations financières* and to 400,000 for the councils of *douars*. The number of Muslim departmental councillors rose from six to nine, in other words to a quarter of the membership of the *conseils généraux*, while the proportion of Muslim municipal councillors, fixed at no more than a quarter since 1884, was raised to one-third. Municipal councillors meanwhile recovered the right to share in the election of the mayor. In the end it was a very timid package against which the mayors of Algeria protested loud and long, and certainly did not keep the promises made in 1914. The Young Algerians were bitterly disappointed. What no one noticed was that by refusing the Muslim population all right of representation in Paris, even indirect, by creating purely Algerian voters, these reforms simply opened the way to an Algerian citizenship.

In the following years, the Young Algerian movement became split because of its frustration at these measures. Some members favoured naturalisation with the loss of their personal status as Muslims, while others demanded either citizenship or at least some elected representation in parliament while remaining legally Muslim. The former quite straightforwardly expressed the desire of the *évolués* for equality; the latter were more sensitive to the wish of the mass of *indigènes* to keep their faith by keeping what remained of their laws. The latter found a standard bearer in the person of Abd el-Kader's grandson, the 'Emir' Khaled. Although the programme he set out in a weekly paper, *Iqdām* ('Audacity'), was essentially assimilationist, calling for the *departements* to be placed directly under Paris, for an end to the *communes mixtes* and all special native laws, and for six Muslim deputies and three senators, the Algerian administration opposed him as a 'native nationalist', and procured first his electoral defeat and then his exile. Returning to Paris in 1924 in the hope of a hearing from the newly-formed *Cartel des Gauches* or left-wing coalition government, he was again disappointed, and made contact instead with the North African Communists. Condemned to

imprisonment by a French consular tribunal at Alexandria,
where he was arrested on a charge of possessing a false pass-
port, he was obliged to spend the rest of his life in Damascus,
where he died in 1936. In September 1924, after his departure from the scene, the future '*Etoile Nord-Africaine*' ('North
African Star') of Messali Hadj was founded in Paris. In Algeria
itself the Young Algerians, left with few outlets in the press
in the form of the weekly *Taqaddum* ('Progress'), *La Tribune*
and *Le Trait d'Union* ('The Link'), nevertheless extended their
audience. They did so thanks to new leaders, notably Ferhat
Abbas and BenDjelloul. What all of them wanted was the transformation of 'the colony into a province'.

The Europeans, who had never accepted the legislation of
'Jonnart the Muslim' in 1919, which had been 'passed outside
Algeria by assemblies incompetent to do so', continued to claim
the right to govern Algeria themselves through an Algerian
assembly, 'an institution which will allow the laws we need and
want to be passed here in the country'. French governments,
however, preferred to satisfy such aspirations themselves by
reintroducing the *Code de l'indigénat* in 1920 and 1922, and granting a loan of 1,600 million frs. for a programme of large-scale
public works. Of this the lion's share was earmarked for the
irrigation of settler land and the modernisation of the railways.
Still at the request of the *colons*, who wanted to prevent the
departure of Algerian workers to France because it reduced the
work-force and pushed up wages, the governor-general, Chautemps, decided on 8 August 1924 to prohibit the embarkation
of Muslim workers without a work contract.[11]

Governing in this way, solely in accordance with the views
of European Algeria, France may have quietened the *colons* for
a while, but it lost the ear of the Muslims. In 1923 Lyautey,
the great French resident-general in command of the French
Protectorate in Morocco, called it 'a simply criminal policy.'
A radical governor-general, Viollette, became speedily convinced of this, but if he gave back a little hope to the Young

[11] The number of North African workers living in France increased steadily
from 52,000 in 1921 to 70,000 in 1922 and 92,000 in 1923. Representatives
of the *colons* warned that with 'the millions swiped from France' the natives
were buying back good *colon* land . . .

Algerians, he greatly alarmed the Europeans. When, after the rejection of his budget by the *délégations financières* because it proposed a contribution to the French military effort, he spoke of granting the native élite the right to vote along with the French, the powerful Algerian deputies, Thomson and Morinaud, had 'Viollette the Arab' recalled immediately by the prime minister, Poincaré, on 9 November 1927. Viollette then appealed to public opinion. As a member of parliament, he tabled a bill on the occasion of the centenary of French Algeria in 1930 to grant citizenship to the Muslim élite. It was a proposal that obsessed Algeria for the next seven years. In his prophetic book published in 1931, *L'Algérie vivra-t-elle?* ('Will Algeria Survive')? Viollette himself declared that if Algeria were to remain the exclusive fief of the *colons*, it would be lost to France 'in twenty years':

> In fifteen or twenty years, there will be more than 10 million natives in Algeria, of whom about one million men and women will be steeped in French culture. Are we going to make them rebels or Frenchmen? Will we be so blinded by what some people consider to be their immediate material interest that we will sacrifice our African empire and the fate of the country for them? [. . .] If so, and if the Metropole does not intervene to insist on a more just and more humane point of view, Algeria is doomed.

Recalling the demands of the Young Algerians, he explained what he meant: 'If France commits the unpardonable offence of not understanding them, they will be drawn, as in Indo-China, into angry nationalism.' Events were not slow to prove him right.

Part III
'WILL ALGERIA SURVIVE?'
(1930–1954)

6
THE ECONOMIC AND SOCIAL
DEVELOPMENT OF ALGERIA, 1930–1954

The principal features of economic and social change in the twenty-five years that remained before the truth of Viollette's prediction became apparent can be grouped under four heads. In the first place, a massive increase in the Muslim population contrasted with the slow increase among the Europeans. At the same time the retreat of European settlement — the withdrawal of the European population from the land it had colonised with so much effort — was followed by a steady Arab takeover of the countryside and the small towns of the interior. Thirdly, this takeover of the rural area was accompanied by the growing urbanisation of the Muslim population and a rapid increase in the number of '*évolués*'. Finally, the gap between the two sectors of the Algerian economy — on the one hand the modern sector, almost entirely European, and the traditional, Muslim, sector — continued to widen. This dualism of the economy meant that the country was torn relentlessly to pieces at a time when the two societies were coming a little closer together in terms of their material aspirations, at least, if not in their lifestyles.

The European Population

With French immigration almost at a standstill, the European population nevertheless continued to grow at a rate of 1 per cent a year, so that the figure of 833,000 in 1926, including 657,000 French and naturalised French and 176,000 foreigners, had risen to 881,600 in 1931 and 984,000 in 1954, by which time some 70 per cent had been born in Algeria and considered themselves first and foremost as Algerians, whatever their origins. The assimilation of foreigners progressed just as rapidly, and the youngest declared themselves to be nothing but French. While they might be fellow-countrymen, the 'French of France', on the other hand, were regarded as different. As for the Jews of Algeria, who numbered around 140,000 in 1954, they were still regarded with suspicion by the European population despite the remarkable extent of their assimilation, at least until the creation of the state of Israel in 1948. The hostility of the Arab world contrived to silence the anti-Semitism of the Europeans and the Jews' complaints. The unity of French society in Algeria had been achieved.

Economically, 14.4 per cent of the active European population belonged to the primary or agricultural sector, 28.6 per cent to the secondary or industrial sector, and the remaining 57 per cent to the tertiary sector of commerce and services; but once again it is the first of these that catches the eye. The European agricultural population, which had been constantly in decline since the turn of the century, fell to 125,300 in 1948 and 93,000 in 1954 as the concentration of European properties in ever fewer hands was yet further accelerated in the years after 1930. In that year, there had been 26,153 estates or farms of which 5,411 were of more than 100 ha.; in 1940 there were 25,337, with 6,345 over 100 ha. By 1954, colonisation controlled 2,726,000 ha. divided among 22,037 farms or plots, of which 7,432 were of less than 10 ha. In contrast, there were 6,385 cultivators who between them owned no less than 2,381,900 ha. or 87 per cent of the total, and accounted for 70 per cent of gross returns. This meant that since 1930, mechanised estates had grown in number by 18 per cent and in area by 38 per cent, at the expense of medium-to-small European farms. As a result the number of owners had fallen by more than half, from 34,821 in 1930 to 17,129 in 1954. The proportion of those who rented their farms or managed them on a profit-sharing basis had declined from 16 to 10 per cent, while the percentage of salaried personnel, managers and farm workers was down from 43 per cent of the European rural population in 1930 to 25 per cent. But the real seriousness of a situation in which 25 per cent of all the cultivated land in Algeria belonged to 2 per cent of the total agricultural population was clearly in relation to the much greater mass of native society; all countries dominated by great estates have always called for agrarian reform.

On the level of production, meanwhile, European agriculture benefited from a policy of credit and a vast programme of irrigation to achieve a remarkable modernisation between 1930 and 1954. Although land under irrigation was still only 42,000 ha. out of a possible 95,500 ha., the cultivation techniques used for cereals, vineyards and citrus fruits made considerable progress. Mechanisation itself increased beyond all expectation after 1948, each combine harvester eliminating a hundred agricultural labourers. Vineyards grew rapidly from 226,000 ha. in 1929 to 400,000 ha. in 1935, while wine production almost doubled from an annual average of 9,265,000 hectolitres[1] between 1920 and 1929 to one of 17,100,000 hl. between 1930 and 1938. Its decline from 1941 to 1947 was only temporary, and thereafter wine surpassed its pre-war peak with 18,300,000 hl. in 1953 and 19,300,000 hl. in 1954. In spite of increased marketing problems, the companies of the wine industry continued to invest, pushing up yields and increasing output. The great viticultural estates comprised 4,425 properties or 15 per cent of the total number of vineyards, but covered 226,500 ha. or 72 per cent of the total area, and produced more than three-quarters of the Algerian harvest. The vine continued to provide the main income of Algerian agriculture, realising 55 billion frs. in 1953.[2]

Meanwhile European grain covered 28 per cent of the area given over to cereals and accounted for 44 per cent of Algeria's total production. Advances in cultivation between 1950 and 1954, extending to the more marginal land, drove this production back up to its historic peak before the First World War, between 1909 and 1913. Even more spectacular was the development of early vegetables and citrus fruits. The production of the latter increased from 100,000 tonnes before the war to 340,000 tonnes in 1954, with a value of 6 billion frs. In terms of the country as a whole, an agriculture which

---

[1] 1 hectolitre, abbreviation hl., = 100 litres.
[2] These are the so-called 'old' francs of the post-war period of massive devaluation. 100 'old' francs = 1 'new' franc, introduced in 1958.

involved less than 10 per cent of the European population accounted for 55 per cent of the value of total Algerian agricultural production, animal and plant combined, and no less than 66 per cent of the value of crops alone. In terms of the stock exchange, by 1954 the rural estates of European colonisation represented a capital of some 600 billion frs. yielding a net annual income of 93 billion. For the landowners and for the shareholders of the companies involved, this was the golden age.

The ebbing away of the European rural population induced by this massive concentration of agricultural property meant a flow back into the towns and especially into the few great cities. The European urban population went up from 673,000 in 1931 to 792,000 in 1954, when 80 per cent of all Europeans lived in forty-six towns, and half of these in Algiers and Oran. For such as these, the non-agricultural sector of the economy likewise made considerable progress, contributing two-thirds of Algeria's national product. Three-quarters of this was accounted for by 15,000 European companies, the rest by 150,000 small businesses, of which 50,000 were non-Muslim. Here again it was a tale of growing concentration and expansion on the part of the companies involved, which is easily traced. In 1937, 667 European businesses had a combined workforce of 51,652, while by 1958 the 668 firms whose staffs had risen to more than fifty had a total of 94,103 employees. As a result, the urban Europeans became increasingly a population of salary-earners at the middle and upper levels of employment; in 1954 the number of these was 253,000, of both sexes. The number of European manual workers and domestics was no higher in 1954 than it had been before 1914, while managers, civil servants and office workers had multiplied by 2.6, and heads of businesses and self-employed persons by 1.9. But the development was not properly balanced, for the excessive size of the commercial sector, with tradesmen at 16 per cent and small craftsmen at 6 per cent of the whole, was typical of what became known as a 'third world' society.

Nevertheless, the European population quite clearly formed the dominant society of Algeria, supplying 92.8 per cent of managers, 82.4 per cent of technicians and foremen, and 86 per cent of civil servants. Although within itself it was quite sharply stratified, for the most part it enjoyed a high standard of living, statistically described as 'middle-class' for 560,000 people in 1951. The costs of summer holidays outside Algeria for 187,000 Europeans alone came to about 20 billion old francs.

The Muslim Population

The growth of the Muslim population, caused by the fall in the death rate, stands out as a determinant of the period 1930–54, a population explosion calling for economic and political action. Far from obtaining it, the demographic revolution simply went to increase still further the imbalances of society and the economy. The so-called municipal Muslim population, i.e. the vast majority who lived in the various *communes*, rose from 5,150,000 in 1926 to 5,588,000 in 1931, and reached 8,450,000 in 1954 (this total would reach some 8,700,000 if temporary emigrants to France are included). The rate of increase involved went up from around 1.4 per cent a year before 1914 to 2.85 per cent in 1954, compared to Egypt's 1.84 per cent. As a result the Muslim Algerian population was one of the youngest in the world, with 52.6 per cent under the age of twenty, and 100 children under fourteen to every ninety-four 'adults'. More than two-thirds still lived at the level of a pre-capitalist subsistence economy, an immense traditional peasantry who now lacked the crops or the livestock to maintain the traditional way of life. The total annual grain production, European and native, that averaged 19.6 million quintals in 1901–10, decreased to 16 million between 1921 and 1930 and to 14 million between 1941 and 1948; it did no more than return to an average of 19.7 million quintals between 1948 and 1954 — largely, as we have seen, because of the European effort. Similarly the number of sheep, which was about 8,900,000 before 1910, had fallen to 5,300,000 in the 1920s and 4,800,000 in the 1940s, rising only slightly to 5 million between 1948 and 1954. Also, the production of olive oil, which had averaged about 350,000 hl. between 1910 and 1920, dropped to 165,000 hl. in the 1930s and rose to only 212,000 hl. in 1951–2.

This general decline in output at a time when the population was rising can be explained by economic factors — by a decrease in the area owned and cultivated by Muslims from 7,562,977 ha. in 1930 to 7,349,100 ha. in 1950, by its continual parcelling out into smaller and smaller plots, and by the stagnation of yields and the degradation of the soils. After 1930, land in Muslim ownership was on the one hand concentrated at the expense of the smaller properties, and on the other divided up at the expense of the medium-sized. In 1950, therefore, there were 438,483 Muslim properties of less than 10 ha., covering in all 1,378,000 ha., and 167,170 properties averaging 19 ha. and covering 3,185,000 ha. Between them they accounted for about 43 per cent of the total area compared to 35 per cent in 1930. Conversely, there were 16,580 properties averaging 66 ha. and covering 1,096,000 ha., which was now only 14.9 per cent of the total area compared to 16 per cent in 1930. Meanwhile, at the very top, 1,688,800 ha. were divided among 8,499 properties with an average of 200 ha. each. To appreciate these figures, it must be remembered that Muslim properties rarely had a single tenant, some four-fifths being divided up into small plots; that two-year periods of fallow to allow for grazing remained the normal practice; that one in two farms had no other agricultural equipment than the wooden plough; and that agricultural credit for such smallholdings was unknown. This explains why the average yields of native crops did not exceed 4.65 quintals of grain per hectare over the years 1945–54, compared to an average of 6 quintals per hectare between 1905 and 1914. The threshold of malnutrition being variously estimated by region and by year at the level of a farm of between 12 and 20 ha., it can be seen that two-thirds of the *fellahs* formed not an independent peasantry but a class of semi-proletarians. All in all, no more than 20,000 farmers belonged to the modern agricultural sector of the economy, while the annual *per capita* income of the Muslim cultivator was reckoned as low as 22,000 old frs. (£22 or $66 at the then current rate of exchange).

It is more difficult, using the unreliable or contradictory statistics available, to pursue this analysis of the composition of rural Algerian society. By 1950 no more than 9 or 10 per cent would have been *khammes* or sharecroppers and 12 per cent pastoralists. Farm labourers, permanent and temporary, would have accounted for 22 per cent in 1954, peasant proprietors for

19.5 per cent. It would certainly be unwise to rely too heavily on these percentages, but when compared with those for 1930 and 1910, they do provide a measure of the changes that had undoubtedly taken place, notably the great reduction in the numbers of pastoralists and sharecroppers, sharecropping itself being well on the way to extinction. More unexpected is the smallness of the increase in agricultural wage labour, which is probably to be explained by the growing mechanisation of European farming. The outstanding phenomenon, which does not appear directly in these figures, is the enormous number of those out of work and unemployed. In 1955 the Delavignette report of the commission of enquiry in 1954 put the total number of unemployed in the rural sector at 400,000. Depending on the source, the figure rises to anything between 650,000 and 850,000 if one includes the underemployed, sometimes called 'family helps'. Yet other statistics speak of a million out of work in the countryside in 1954, at a time when there were no more than 112,000 'permanent' agricultural workers, those who worked at least 180 days a year for wages which traditionally were the lowest for any kind of labour.

In these circumstances the size of the rural exodus is easily explained. The exodus itself took various forms, with people from the *bled*[3] or countryside coming into the European farming districts and into the towns, and going on as temporary emigrants to metropolitan France. A continuous stream of internal migration began by bringing the rural Muslim population down from the high barren plains or the overpopulated mountains into the prosperous regions occupied by the Europeans. Between 1925 and 1948, for example, the population of the Mitidja rose from 80,000 to about 250,000. Thereafter this immigration was no longer possible, and the towns took the brunt of the flight from the land. But these rapidly proved unable to offer any adequate relief. Between 1936 and 1954 the Muslim urban population rose from 722,000 to about 1,600,000; this was an increase from 11.6 per cent of the total native population in 1936 to 14.7 per cent in 1948 and 18.9 per cent in 1954. Packed into the traditional Arab quarters of the cities or clustered into *bidonvilles* (shanty towns) on the outskirts,

---

[3] Arabic *bilād*.

this population was soon unable any longer to find work in spite of the steady growth in the number of jobs.

Factories and workshops employed 110,000 workers in 1924 and 264,000 in 1954, while European businesses in general employed some 320,000. In the whole of the non-agricultural sector, there were by then about 120,000 independent Muslim workers and 463,187 wage-earners. The former were crafts-men or small tradesmen with fewer than 30,000 employees; the net earnings of some 100,000 Muslim businesses came to no more than 33 billion frs., compared to the 375 billion frs. of some 65,000 European enterprises. As for the wage-earners in industry, commerce and public employment, there were 133,110 out of work, 172,000 unskilled labourers of whom 84,000 were partially unemployed, and 75,000 skilled workers; 68,000 were professionals, minor civil servants or other employees, while there were 12,000 in managerial or technical positions. Muslims thus constituted 95 per cent of the unskilled labour force and 68 per cent of the skilled, but only 17.6 per cent of those in technical grades and 7.2 per cent of executives. The evident saturation of the urban labour market represented by these figures brought about the large-scale resumption of emigration to metropolitan France, which had fallen off in the 1930s but rose after 1948 to an unprecedented level. This short-term emigration of between two and four years on the part of young men from the countryside involved about 300,000 in 1954, one adult male in seven. The same number of families remaining in the *douars* lived essentially on the money they remitted. At 33 billion frs., these remittances in 1954 repre-sented a sum equivalent to the to.al wages paid in Algerian agriculture.

Faced with this problem the Algerian administration, lack-ing initiative, ill-equipped and ill-informed in such economic matters, could find no way to deal with it. Medium- and long-term credit remained as difficult as ever for the *fellah* to obtain. The SIPs (*Sociétés Indigènes de Prévoyance* or Native Provident Societies), introduced as long ago as 1893 under the Cambon administration, failed to modernise themselves in spite of the creation of a common fund for their benefit in 1933; during the war they were merely amalgamated, bringing the number down from 260 in 1940 to 107 in 1946. In 1952, when they were transformed into the SAPs (*Sociétés Agricoles de Prévoyance* or Agricultural Provident Societies), their budget was increased, but they still permitted only modest, short-term loans. On that basis, at least, they involved the bulk of the landowning peasantry, 500,000 of whom were clients of 105 societies in 1954.

More ambitiously, in 1937, for the first time since the attempts made by the *bureaux arabes* in the middle of the nineteenth century, the active development of the rural economy was proposed. Although this 'native peasantry' programme led only to a few individual undertakings, these prompted the new governor-general Yves Chataigneau to introduce a much grander scheme in 1946, no less than a whole new institution, the *Secteur d'Amélioration Rurale* (Rural Improvement Sector or SAR). Here the intention was to bring the peasants of a particular sector or district into a cooperative society with the necessary credit and agricultural machinery to modernise the traditional economy. Under the initial plan, there were to have been 800 SARs by 1956, covering the whole country. By the beginning of 1948 there were already 103, involving 75,000 families, but after 1948 their growth was halted; they were subordinated to the feeble SIPs and associated with large private estates. Thus they ceased to concern the mass of the Muslim population for whom they had been established. By 1954 there were only 133 agricultural SARs, eighty-one for cereals, forty-six for tree crops and six for the desert oases, covering 2,580,000 ha. and involving 201,000 *fellahs*; the sixty-seven SARs for livestock concerned only 103,000 pastoralists. The problem of the land itself was considered insoluble. Various attempts by the administration to find 'resettlement areas' for the landless poor all failed. The Martin law of 1942, which aimed to redistribute 15 per cent of all irrigated land to the small cultivator, was never applied; the expropriation of great estates, foreign-owned or not, which was frequently mentioned as a possibility, simply could not be brought about. The thirty-three estates of over 2000 ha., the 15,000 ha. of the Compagnie Génévoise and the 70,000 ha. of the Compagnie Algérienne remained intact. No study of agrarian reform was undertaken.

A policy of industrialisation was decided upon in 1946 within the framework of the 'Muslim reforms' announced at Constantine in 1943.[4] After a rapid start it slowed down considerably, and the five-year industrialisation plan was never implemented. In all, only 15,000 new jobs had been created by the end of 1954; the Muslim population scarcely noticed. Down to 1954 professional training, which lies at the root of all economic development, was not considered a key problem and was not made the object of any general policy or plan. Education proceeded without any such concern, barely ahead of the rise in population. In 1930, only 68,000 Muslim children attended state primary schools; by 1944 the number had risen to 110,000 and by 1954 to 302,000, the proportion increasing from 5 per cent to 8.8 and then 14 per cent. Secondary education went to a mere 1,358 Muslims in 1940 and to 6,260 in 1954; the numbers in higher education were 89 and 589. It should come as no surprise, therefore, that in 1954 the Algerian élite, besides being badly distributed among the professions with 354 advocates and notaries but only twenty-eight engineers, was so very small, with 185 secondary teachers and 165 doctors, dentists and pharmacists; nor that 90 per cent of the population was illiterate.

These modest figures, however, should not obscure the profound transformation that had taken place in the way of life and outlook of a far greater number of Muslims. The extent and rapidity of the change cannot be measured simply in terms of French or Arabic schooling. The influence on the men of the time they had spent in metropolitan France has to be appreciated. Over a forty-year period, from 1914 to 1954, no less than two million Muslim Algerians had lived in France either as soldiers or as workers. Within Algeria itself the fact of living side by side with Europeans in the towns, even if the two societies did not mix, was equally important, especially perhaps for the women, who through their work and through the radio became familiar with the European way of life and began to envy it. In ways like these, the humblest experienced the social and economic juxtaposition of the two Algerias: a modern Algeria in the process of development and getting rich, and a traditional, underdeveloped Algeria sinking further and further into poverty. This awareness at the level of needs and

[4] See below, pp. 100–1.

aspirations fundamentally changed the way in which the two
civilisations lived side by side; the differences became ine-
qualities and injustices.

As matters stood in 1954, therefore, Algeria was a prey to
insoluble difficulties: the monopoly of land-ownership by a
minority, paucity of investment, the absence of an internal
market and of any kind of economic policy for the future. All
these pointed to the deepening of a crisis made all the more
tragic by the rapid increase in the Muslim population and the
decline in its standard of living. It is easy to understand why
some of those responsible for the government of the country
were calling for France to take complete control of Algeria as
the only way out of the morass. But as a solution such integration was virtually ruled out in advance by the political
development of the Muslims.

7

THE POLITICAL DEVELOPMENT OF ALGERIA, 1930–1954

'Will Algeria survive?' The reply to Viollette's question, for the Muslims, consisted entirely in the birth and development of Algerian nationalism, accelerated by the effects of the Second World War. As far as the Europeans were concerned, political life went through more or less the same stages as in France, without affecting their stance on the local issue. European Algerians declared themselves aggressively 'Algerians' in any conflict with metropolitan France, and resolutely French in any conflict with the Muslims. The combination of elderly politicians and the agricultural interest[1] set the tone, and went far to perpetuate this short-sighted parochialism.

The Birth of Algerian Nationalism

The centenary of the French conquest in 1930, celebrated in humiliating fashion for the Muslims, may be taken as the moment when the alienation of the Algerian élite set in. Up until then, this élite had thought only in terms of French citizenship in its struggle for equality. Now another way forward was proclaimed by Messali Hadj, by the Algerian *'ulamā'* or *oulema*, and by the champions of Arabism, of whom the Emir Chekib Arslan was the most active and persistent.[2]

In Paris, a Communist organisation of North African workers was founded in March 1926 under the name *Étoile Nord-Africaine* (ENA — North African Star). In the following

---

[1] The *colons* proper, those with land, had 24 delegates to the *délégations financières*, elected by 19,000 voters; other Europeans had a further 24, chosen by 78,000 electors; Muslims had 21 delegates representing 112,000 electors. Out of these 69 delegates, no less than 53 represented the interests of the big estates.

[2] The Lebanese Chekib Arslan was head of the permanent delegation of the Syro-Palestinian Committee at the League of Nations in Geneva, and editor of the influential *La Nation Arabe*.

year, however, it fell under the direction of Messali Hadj, who turned it into a nationalist movement fighting for Algerian independence and social revolution. Its newspapers, the bilingual *Iqdam nord-africain* (North African Enterprise), followed by *El Oumma* (The Muslim People); its participation in the Anti-Colonial Congress held in Brussels in 1927; and its open letters to the League of Nations — all of these advertised the movement to Algerian workers in France, of whom there were 40,000 in 1931. In Algeria itself it only took root in August 1936, but then developed rapidly into the *Parti du Peuple Algérien* (PPA — Algerian People's Party), which was formed in March 1937. The leading militants were almost immediately arrested, but by 1938 the party had 2,500 members.

Meanwhile, in Algeria itself the initiative had fallen to three *oulema* who had studied outside the country. These were Abd el-Hamid Ben Badis from Constantine, Tayyib el-Okbi from Algiers, and Bachir el-Ibrahimi from Tlemcen. In conformity with the classic formula of the movement for Islamic reform, which went back to Muḥammad 'Abduh in Egypt at the turn of the century, these men undertook to restore the faith to its original purity while reasserting the Arabic character of a country menaced by the spread of the French language and culture. To this end they set their face against 'maraboutism, the accomplice of colonialism', and set out to train a new generation of leaders in Arab culture. From May 1931 thirteen of them, including Mubarak el-Mili and Tewfik el-Madani, the first authors of national histories of Algeria written in Arabic, came together in an Association of Reforming 'Ulamā' or *Muṣliḥīn*. Nationalism proper had been born. The patriotic history of Shaykh el-Madani, *Kitāb al-Jazā'ir*, lit. 'Book of Algiers', 'printed at the expense of the Algerian nation' in 1931, carried on its cover the motto of the reforming *oulema*: 'Islam is our religion, Algeria is our country, Arabic is our language.' Several words with new meanings appeared in Algerian Arabic, such as *watan*, homeland or fatherland; *al-umma al-jazā'iriyya*, the Algerian nation; and *al-sha'b*, the people. However, with its Islamic and Arabic character this new-found Algerian nationalism was at the same time part of the much wider Arab renaissance, directly linked to the international Arab-Islamic movement and in full agreement with the resolutions of the First

Congress of Jerusalem in December 1931.[3] The association
expounded its doctrines in a number of reviews, such as *Al-
Shihāb* (the Meteor), founded by Ben Badis in 1924; *Al-Sunna*
(The Way of the Prophet); *Al-Sharī'a al-Muṭahhara* (The Puri-
fied Law of God); and *Al-Basā'ir*, (Visions of the Future).
These concentrated their attack upon the cult of saints, the
religious brotherhoods, and 'all reprehensible innovations' in
religion. Various popular papers, even more aggressive in their
tone, survived only a short time.

Members of the association preached both in the mosques,
which as a result were closed to them in 1933, and privately.
Most of their effort, however, was directed towards the creation
of primary schools and free *medersas* teaching modern subjects
in Arabic. These private schools, sometimes tolerated, and
sometimes closed by the administration under a law of 8 March
1938, numbered ninety in 1947 and 181 in 1954, including fifty-
eight *medersas*, with 40,000 pupils. They were above all schools
of patriotism which strove to inspire in their pupils a sense of
their grand ideal: 'Live for Islam and Algeria.' While initially
keeping out of politics, the *oulema* often took sides, especially
against Muslim advocates of assimilation. The famous 'Clear
statement' of April 1936 was made in reply to the equally
celebrated statement of Ferhat Abbas in February, that Algeria
existed only as part of France:

> We the *oulema*, speaking in the name of the majority of
> natives of this country, say to those who claim to be French:
> 'You do not represent us! . . . the Muslim population of
> Algeria has its own history, religious unity, language, culture
> and traditions . . . *This Muslim population is not part of France,
> cannot be part of France, and does not want to be part of France.*

It cannot be doubted that in the climate of growing opposition
between 1933 and 1936, the *oulema* had firmly established their
influence and won over Muslim opinion to their cause.

On the other hand the Young Algerians, supporters of

[3] Called by the Grand Mufti of Jerusalem as a result of the serious clashes
between Arabs and Jews in Palestine in 1929, the Congress was a dramatic
step towards the formulation of an Arab nationalist ideology.

assimilation, could achieve nothing despite the formation in 1927 of a *Fédération des Élus Indigènes* by Dr Ben Djelloul and Ferhat Abbas. Their audience, which was in any case restricted to the lower middle classes and the *évolués*, dwindled with each setback. They encountered strong opposition from a governor-general born in Algeria, Jules Carde, and had their full share of disappointment. In 1933 the government and the two Chambers of the National Assembly, deputies and senators alike, refused to meet their delegation which had come to Paris to support the Viollette bill of 1931; 950 Muslim *élus* in the various Algerian assemblies resigned as a result. In 1935 the Minister of the Interior, Régnier, refused at the end of a fact-finding visit to Algeria to consider the prospect of any further emancipation. Meanwhile Ferhat Abbas' confidential proposal for the abolition of Muslim personal status in exchange for French citizenship was disclosed to the Senate. Carde's successor, Le Beau, did indeed receive instructions to 'reestablish relations with the native elite', but that had to wait until the formation of the Popular Front government in 1936.

The election of the left-wing Popular Front under the Prime Minister Léon Blum was indeed an occasion for fresh hope by Muslim Algerians. A sympathetic government was at last in power in Paris, while the proposals for electoral reform put forward by the former governor-general, Viollette, encouraged the majority of the Algerian élite to believe that political emancipation and the end of colonial subjection would finally come about through legal equality with the framework of France. With this prospect in view, the *Fédération des Élus*, the *oulema* and the Communists called the First Muslim Congress on 7 June 1936. The political charter which it drew up called for an end to all discriminatory laws and institutions, straightforward unification of Algeria with France, a single electorate, and the representation of Muslims in parliament. At the same time, French citizenship should be compatible with Muslim personal status, while Muslim worship would be freed from state control and supported by the revenues of *habous* or pious endowments.

Such a platform was as unacceptable to the Messalists of the Étoile Nord-Africaine, who demanded independence, as it was to Blum himself, prime minister of the Popular Front but nevertheless the 'loyal manager' of the Empire. What he did was put forward the Viollette bill for the extension of political rights to the Algerian élite, namely officers and non-commissioned officers, graduates and qualified professionals, and public employees. Twenty-one thousand Muslim French would thus have obtained the right to vote with the 202,750 European electors in parliamentary elections, while the parliamentary representation of Algeria would have risen to one deputy for every 20,000 voters. Viollette's aim was to force the European population to find in this single electorate common ground on which to come to an agreement with the Europeanised element in native Algerian society, whose enthusiasm for the proposal carried away both the Algerian Communist Party and the *oulema*. Only the new *Parti du Peuple Algérien* of Messali Hadj continued to oppose the bill, which it claimed was intended 'to break up the Muslim community' by the creation of a privileged minority. From the French point of view it was certainly true that this desirable extension of citizenship would have been the most effective obstacle to Algerian nationalism, as the report on the bill by the Lagrosillière parliamentary sub-committee made clear.

But in Algeria such considerations were lost in the general outcry of the European population, in particular the mayors, councillors and deputies: 'The entry of Muslims into the electoral body', said Marshal Juin, 'would naturally undermine their personal position.' Algeria's members of parliament, and then its mayors, announced that they would resign *en bloc* if the bill went through; rather more wily politicians declared themselves in favour of a dual electorate or the establishment in Paris of a purely consultative Muslim High Committee. The conservative press in France encouraged the resistance of the *colons*, and Léon Blum did not dare to reform Algeria by decree. In spite of an urgent appeal by the Second Muslim Congress in 1937, *the Blum-Viollette bill was never even discussed by parliament.* Having increased the number of native delegates to the *Délégations financières* by decree from twenty-one to twenty-four, or half the number of forty-eight European members, Albert Sarraut, Minister of the Interior in the subsequent Chautemps and Daladier governments, proved equally incapable of persuading the European *élus* of Algeria to give up their campaign of obstruction: 'I have to admit that these gentlemen have neither patriotism, nor heart, nor reason.' The abandonment of the Blum-Viollette bill sounded the death-knell of the policy of assimilation; and the dashing of hope was heavy with menace. Dr Ben Djelloul immediately came to the conclusion that the historian is obliged to draw in retrospect: 'Muslim Algerians will reserve the right to demand something else.'

Algeria during the Second World War

The war with Nazi Germany and the defeat of France had no immediate effect on the Muslim population. Authoritarian and backward-looking, the 'National Revolution' of Marshal Pétain's Vichy government charmed the French of Algeria. Nor did it in fact displease the Muslims, who had good memories of Napoleon III, despised the parliamentary regime, and hated 'the Republic of the *colons*'. The first measures of the Vichy government tended to reinforce this unexpected unanimity. On 7 October 1940 Peyrouton, the new Minister of the Interior and former secretary-general to the government in Algiers, abolished the Crémieux decree of 1870 naturalising the Algerian Jews, and on 11 October he deprived them of the right to seek naturalisation. Peyrouton, a strenuous opponent of Muslim demands in Tunis as well as Algiers, thus provided himself with yet another argument against any extension of French citizenship, while satisfying the instinctive anti-Semitism of European Algerians.

However, lacking the knee-jerk reflex of colonialism in these matters, Pétain gave equal representation to Europeans and Muslims from Algeria in the National Council he created in January 1941.[4] Despite the fact that the abolition of the *Conseils généraux* and the *délégations financières* had deprived their leaders of their status as elected representatives, the Muslim *élus* responded. Ferhat Abbas' letter of 10 April 1941 was a final attempt to win from a government freed from all parliamentary obstruction a programme of reform capable of giving 'six million orientals' the will to live side by side with the Algerian

---

[4] Although Admiral Abrial, the governor-general, contrived to select only four Muslims as against five Europeans.

French. To this, however, Vichy merely replied four months later that it would take note of his suggestions. It had no intention of addressing itself to the political problem, but it did at least promulgate the Martin law[5] to expropriate a proportion of the lands brought under cultivation within the area irrigated by the state dams, for the purpose of resettling the *fellahs*.

Defeat, however, had ruined the prestige of France. Official propaganda revelled in masochism; demobilised soldiers and freed prisoners of war spoke of the 'farce of a war'. In comparison, the successes of Germany evoked a certain admiration. Meanwhile the economic situation deteriorated rapidly, and the harvests diminished. With little industry, Algeria lacked fertiliser, manufactured goods and clothing. New suffering overwhelmed the poor.

After the Anglo-American landings of 8 November 1942, assisted by a handful of the French Resistance, the political situation, at least, changed radically. Algerian Muslims were introduced to American power and American diplomats, prodigal with their promises and anti-colonial declarations. Abbas and his friends made contact with them, and proceeded to develop a federal concept of Franco-Algerian relations. In response to the appeals of Admiral Darlan, the Vichy leader who unexpectedly brought Algeria over to the Allies, and General Giraud, who took command after his murder, for a great military effort on the part of the Muslims, they replied on 20 December 1942 with a 'Message to the responsible authorities', in other words the Anglo-American High Command; it was not sent 'to the French authorities' until two days later. In it they subordinated the war effort to the meeting of a purely Muslim assembly to draw up a new political, social and economic plan for the country, and to a clear undertaking by France to accept the result. Neither Giraud nor Peyrouton, now appointed governor-general, replied. Ferhat Abbas thereupon drew up a document which, in spite of appearances, was rather less curt and specific: the *Manifeste du Peuple Algérien* (Manifesto of the Algerian People). On 31 March 1943 this was accepted by Peyrouton, so as not to hinder the general mobilisation, 'as the basis of reforms to come'. Fifty-six Muslim notables or

[5] See above, p. 90.

élus were allowed to add their signatures, while to gain time a 'Committee of Muslim Studies' was set up. But on 26 May the Muslim delegates to a preliminary session of the old *délégations financières* drew up a precise political agenda in the form of a 'Programme of Reforms following on from the Manifesto'. This so-called *'Additif* (Supplement) proposed that at the end of the war Algeria would be erected into 'an autonomous Algerian state after the meeting of a Constituent Assembly elected by all the inhabitants of Algeria'. Meanwhile, the old government-general would be transformed into an Algerian government consisting of ministers divided equally between French and Muslims under the presidency of a French ambassador in the role of High Commissioner.

This plan of reform, hardly acceptable to a colonial power, was duly rejected by General Catroux, Peyrouton's successor as governor-general, who had been appointed by the *Comité Francaise de la Libération National* (CFLN), that is the new Free French government of France formed at Algiers on 3 June 1943 under the presidency of Generals de Gaulle and Giraud. Instead, he settled for six timid ordinances. On 22 September 1943, when the *Délégations financières* that had been suspended since 1939 met for their first full session, the Muslim delegates abstained from taking their seats. A new Committee of Muslim Reforms was nevertheless put together, and set to work — for the first time seriously — to draft the reforms which General de Gaulle announced in his Constantine Speech of 12 December 1943. Passing over the opposition of the French in Algeria, who refused to accept these 'surrenders', as well as the objections of constitutional lawyers, the General in his capacity as President of the CFLN announced the grant of French citizenship to some tens of thousands of Muslims who would nevertheless still enjoy their Muslim personal status. It was, in fact, the fulfilment of the promise of the Viollette bill, but 'it was too late'. The nationalist leaders Messali, Ibrahimi and Abbas unanimously rejected this policy of assimilation. It was accepted only by Muslim moderates, the followers of Dr Ben Djelloul, who had signed the Manifesto but refused to go along with the *Additif*; and, for very different reasons, by the Communists. Notwithstanding, on 7 March 1944 de Gaulle signed a decree abolishing the whole apparatus of legal and administrative discrimination against Muslims. It conferred upon them instead all the rights and duties of the French in Algeria, gave them access to all military and civil positions, and increased their representation in the local Algerian assemblies from one-third to two-fifths. The old Muslim electorate was widened to include all persons over the age of twenty-one, a total of 1,500,000, while the French electorate proper, numbering 450,000, was opened to 50–60,000 Muslims falling into sixteen different categories (in practice only 32,000 agreed to be enrolled in this way as first class voters).

From this moment on, a direct struggle for hearts and minds was joined between the French reformers and the Algerian nationalists, one in which Ferhat Abbas occupied the middle ground. To keep the initiative for himself and his programme, he endeavoured to establish a single front with the *oulema* on the one hand and the clandestine PPA, banned more or less since its foundation in 1937, on the other. This was the origin, on 14 March 1944, of the *Amis du Manifeste*, the Association of Friends of the Manifesto and Freedom, whose stated aim was 'to make familiar the idea of an Algerian nation, and to make desirable the creation in Algeria of an autonomous Republic federated to a revived French Republic'. In the difficult economic climate of 1944–5, however, with soaring inflation and the scandal of the black market, the Algerian masses grew far more radical, and the nationalist propaganda of the PPA in favour of an 'Algerian parliament' and an 'Algerian government' easily prevailed over the federalist concept of Abbas. In March 1945, at the First Congress of the Friends of the Manifesto, which by now counted 350,000 members, Messali was hailed as 'the undoubted leader of the Algerian people'.

Troubles in neighbouring Morocco, the constituent meeting of the Arab League, and the preparations for the San Francisco Conference of the new United Nations at which, people were saying, the independence of Algeria would be proclaimed, all led the militants to believe that the hour had come. The deportation of Messali on 25 April did the rest. After tumultuous demonstrations on 1 May 1945, further demonstrations arranged for the day of the German surrender on 8 May turned into armed riots at Sétif and Guelma. In the days after the bloody clashes at these two towns, the small European settlements in the vicinity were attacked. Some 50,000 rioters killed any Europeans they came across, leaving 103 dead, some 100 wounded and mutilated, and many women raped. These were the tragic victims of the revolt of the Constantinois, 8–15 May. They inspired a pitiless repression that fully reflected the fear and hatred on the part of the *colons*. The authorities admitted that they must have killed 1,500 but doubtless the true figure was four or five times higher. Whatever the number, in the eyes of the Algerians a provocation had been followed by an unpardonable massacre. Courts-martial went on to convict 1,476 out of the 4,560 Algerians accused. The Europeans were generally of the opinion that a far greater insurrection had been nipped in the bud, and their elected representatives were quick to use Sétif and Guelma as an argument for the withdrawal of the ordinance of 7 March and the recall of the governor, Chataigneau.

The Progress of Algerian Nationalism, 1945–54

Chataigneau, however, was not recalled, and after the disaster courageously tried to reconstruct a viable Algeria. Economic recovery was slow, but the introduction of the *Secteurs d'amélioration rurale* (SAR), together with a soil restoration agency, was a preparation for the future. A reform of the administration was undertaken and 'municipal centres' were created, gradually to replace the old *communes mixtes* with local Muslim councils. Political reform was taken a step further: a decree of 17 August 1945 for the first time granted the purely Muslim electorate, the so-called 'second college', the right to send the same number of representatives to parliament as the French electors of the 'first college'. Despite such apparent goodwill, the PPA and the Friends of the Manifesto, whose association was dissolved by the government following the events of May 1945, recommended abstention from the elections to the first Constituent Assembly, held in Paris in October 1945 to write the constitution of the new Fourth Republic of France after the war. The abstention, however, was observed only in the towns; and in all 54.48 per cent of eligible Muslims voted, the majority for the friends of Ben Djelloul, who won seven seats, and for the Socialists, who continued to support the policy of assimilation. The proposal of their deputies for the integration of the two electorates was nevertheless rebuffed by the elected European representatives of Algeria as well as by the Algerian Communists, and was not discussed by the Constituent Assembly, which contented itself with voting an amnesty for May 1945 on 16 March 1946.

Ferhat Abbas himself refused to pin his hopes for reform upon de Gaulle's promising new political party, the *Rassemblement du Peuple Français* (RPF), and instead created a new party which this time was his alone, the *Union Démocratique du Manifeste Algérien* (UDMA). The Republic of Algeria which he envisaged was an autonomous but associated member of the *Union française*, the French 'Commonwealth' created in 1946 to replace the old French Empire; it would be fully independent internally while leaving the Union to take care of foreign affairs and defence. The French of Algeria would be recognised as Algerian citizens, in return for which every Algerian citizen would enjoy citizenship in France. The Algerian parliament, directly elected by universal suffrage, would be in control of the budget and enjoy legislative power.

However, as a blueprint for the future, this Algeria had no success. The UDMA deputies, with eleven out of the thirteen Muslim seats in the elections of 1946 to the Second Constituent Assembly, were given a hostile reception by the Assembly itself. 'It is your last chance', said Abbas 'we are the last barrier to secession.' But Edward Herriot, President of the Assembly and elder statesman, simply invited him to 'talk French'. The only decision taken was to increase the number of Muslims entitled to vote with the Europeans in the first electoral college by the law of 5 October 1946. The Second Constituent Assembly wound itself up without even discussing the *Statut de l'Algérie*, the constitutional status of the country, voting instead for a constitutional document in which the fate of Algeria was not specified (although article 60 did speak of a *département d'outre-mer* or overseas *département* like the French West Indies, for example, entitled to send representatives to Paris). Thus when Algeria

voted again in the referendum of October 1946 to approve the
new French constitution and inaugurate the Fourth Republic,
UDMA called for a boycott, and the Muslim turnout was only
39 per cent. As a result, the distribution of seats changed completely. Official candidates, backed by the administration, won
eight seats and the Communists two. The remaining five went
to the followers of Messali Hadj, who since the freeing of their
leader after seven years in detention were now organised in yet
another new party, the *Mouvement pour la Triomphe des Libertés
Démocratiques* (MTLD — Movement for the Triumph of Democratic Freedoms).

In 1947 the new French parliament finally turned to the question of the *Statut de l'Algérie*, left over from the constitutional
deliberations of the previous year. Among the seven drafts proposed by the various French and Algerian parties, not one was
assimilationist, but neither was any in favour of independence,
since the MTLD, not recognising the sovereignty of parliament
in the matter, refused to put forward a submission. Three,
including the Communist proposal, envisaged the status of an
associated state on the grounds that 'the independence of
Algeria would strengthen the foundations of imperialism'. The
French Algerian deputies, opposed to any change, had sub-
mitted no proposal at all, while leaflets and pamphlets had
already begun to circulate in the country declaring that 'Algeria
abandoned by France would have to look after itself', if necessary by an appeal to the United Nations. The government itself
took up the highly conservative version by Georges Bidault in
which Algeria was defined, as in 1900, as a group of *départements*
with its own civil identity and financial autonomy. Executive
power would remain in the hands of a governor-general assisted
by a governmental council, and legislative power with the
National Assembly. The *délégations financières*, which had
changed their name in September 1945 to the *Assemblée financière*
(Financial Assembly), would be dignified with the name of
the Algerian Assembly; its competence would be somewhat
increased but would remain essentially financial. Its decisions
would be subject to the approval of Paris, and if requested, to
the requirement of a two-thirds majority. Representation in the
new Assembly would, in the words of the proposal, be 'equal'
— in other words, sixty delegates each from the two electoral

colleges, in spite of the fact that the first college comprised 464,000 citizens of French civil status, men and women, plus 58,000 Muslims, and the second 1,300,000 Muslims only. Thus, while the scheme had not ventured to repeal the laws which had integrated the Algerian élite into the European population, neither did it dare to make the proposed Algerian Assembly truly representative of the Algerian population, 922,000 Europeans to 7,860,000 Muslims.

The Muslim Algerian deputies, even the moderates, were unanimous in their refusal to countenance such an arrangement, and they withdrew from the debates so as not to be associated with this 'imposition of a constitution'. Even the clauses which provided for real progress, such as an end to the *communes mixtes*, the independence of Muslim worship, the teaching of Arabic at all levels and, in principle at least, the right of Muslim women to vote, were so many empty promises, subject as they would be to the approval of the Algerian Assembly and its impossible requirement of a two-thirds majority. Quite naturally, the Muslims regarded this *Statut du 20 septembre 1947* as an affront; European Algerians, on the other hand, considered it 'a disgrace' (*déshonorant*). In October 1947 this doubly hostile reaction was translated into victory in the municipal elections for the nationalist MTLD and the European *Union algérienne*, each strongly opposed to the *Statut*. The elections for the new Algerian Assembly were therefore put off. Chataigneau, as governor, was considered too weak to deal with the situation by the premier, René Mayer, and was replaced in February 1948 by a Socialist of strongly nationalistic French views, Marcel-Edmond Naegelen. Determined to break the influence of Muslim nationalists, Naegelen ordered his administration to make sure of a 'good election'. And indeed, in April 1948, out of the sixty seats allocated to the Muslim second college, forty-one fell to so-called 'administrative' candidates, only nine to the MTLD, eight to the UDMA and two to independents. All subsequent elections were similar triumphs for the government, deliberate frauds which were repeatedly approved by the parliaments of the Fourth Republic and must therefore be laid at the door of France.

In practising this policy, Governors Naegelen and Léonard drove the Muslims to despair, but won the grateful appreciation

of the French of Algeria. The latter, persuaded that a combination of cunning and strength could maintain the *status quo* indefinitely, made no concessions. When the Algerian Assembly was
finally dissolved in April 1956, it had not even discussed the
tasks assigned to it under the *Statut*. Obliged to provide for
social security, it settled for a minimal scheme passed by fifty-
five out of the 120 votes. Preoccupied with the avoidance of any
increase in direct taxation, the Assembly was incapable of
making the least gesture to the future. Muslim Algeria saw
every legal route to fundamental reform closed off. 'There is
no other solution but the machine-gun', declared Ferhat Abbas
in 1953 as the trial of strength between the nationalists and the
French began in Tunisia and Morocco.

And so the Algerian nationalists increased their support. The
oulema extended their network of schools and influence, shaping
a whole new generation which looked for inspiration to the Arab
east. The UDMA, the party of westernised professionals and
moderates, lost its wide popularity but extended its appeal
upwards to the francophone Muslim élite, while the MTLD
roused the masses in the towns and awoke the peasants to
revolution. The MTLD developed for the purpose a complete
party political organisation directed by permanent officials,
with its own courts, collectors of contributions and agents.
Algeria was divided into five *wilaya* or provinces, thirty-three
daira[6] or circles, and about 100 *qasma*[7] or sections. The underground leaders of the party's OS or *Organisation spécial*, including Ben Bella, Ait Ahmed, Boudiaf and Boussouf, plotted an
armed insurrection. Discovered in 1948 and tracked down over
the next two years, the OS was broken up by the police in 1950
only to be reconstituted with Egyptian assistance. Divisions
nevertheless began to appear. Messali himself, who was
assigned by the police to residence in France in 1952, lost
influence, while the new and liberal mayor of Algiers, Jacques
Chevallier, drew the MTLD members of his council into the
government of the city. The break-up of the party, already a
possibility by 1953, was precipitated by Messali's own short-
sightedness in allowing himself to be elected as president for life

[6] Arabic *dā'ira*, pl. *dawā'ir*.
[7] Arabic *qisma*.

by his personal following in July 1954. The elected members of the MTLD's Central Committee thereupon formed a new 'centralist' party in favour of a broad coalition with other parties. Meanwhile a third splinter, the *Comité Révolutionnaire d'Unité et d'Action* (CRUA —Revolutionary Committee for Unity and Action) was represented by the nine so-called 'historic leaders', almost all of whom were former members of the OS. These determined to bring about the long-planned insurrection as soon as the critical French defeat of Dien Bien Phu in Indo-China on 7 May 1954 became known. The granting of internal self-government to Tunisia following the armed action of the *fellagha*[8] only strengthened their resolve. A tiny secret army called the *Armée de Libération Nationale* (ALN) was set up, and the date of the uprising was fixed for 1 November 1954.

---

[8] 'A local Arabic word for bandits afterwards regarded as a title of honour by the [Tunisian] rebels': Nevill Barbour, ed., *A Survey of North-West Africa (the Maghrib)*, 1st edn, London, New York and Toronto, 1959, 303.

Part IV
THE ALGERIAN WAR

8

THE ALGERIAN INSURRECTION
AND THE FRENCH REACTION
UNDER THE FOURTH REPUBLIC

The outbreak of the insurrection on 1 November 1954 was signalled by a series of terrorist attacks and by the appearance of armed bands, mostly in the Aurès mountains in the southern Constantinois. At the same time, in Cairo, the leaders of the movement announced the founding of the *Front de Libération Nationale* (FLN — National Liberation Front). Considering that after decades of struggle 'the national movement had reached the stage of execution', they proclaimed the start of the revolutionary struggle 'for the liquidation of the colonial system', 'the abandonment of all relics of reformism', and 'national independence through the restoration of the Algerian state'. While offering to negotiate with the French government if it recognised the right to self-determination of every people, including the Algerians whose national identity had for so long been denied, they were primarily concerned to 'internationalise the Algerian question', and declared: 'The struggle will be long but the outcome is certain.' In reply to this manifesto the Minister of the Interior, François Mitterrand, gave the solemn warning that Algeria, centre and heart of the French Republic, guarantee of France's future, would be defended by all possible means. The governor-general immediately dissolved the MTLD and had both Messalist and centralist militants arrested, even though he knew them to be innocent of complicity in the plot. When they were released, as they had to be following the protests of Chevallier, now Minister of Defence in Paris, they hastened to leave Algeria. The centralists joined the FLN, while the diehard Messalists formed a new party, the *Mouvement National Algérien* (MNA). The initial military response was not much happier; even though the government of Mendès-France increased the number of troops from 56,500 to 83,400 in February 1955 by sending in national service conscripts, the army failed to destroy the armed bands. On the contrary, the maltreatment that was meted out to suspects helped them to recruit.

The French premier, Mendès-France, whose determination had brought the war in Vietnam to an end, quite rightly saw the need for more imagination, and for this purpose appointed the Gaullist deputy Jacques Soustelle as Governor. But faced with a hostile reception by the Europeans, who sneered at this 'Jewish native', and confronted by the military, who thought that the army could have no confidence in the nominee of the man who had surrendered Indo-China, Soustelle was slow to come to a decision. Whatever he may have written about himself in his books, the new governor showed little initiative. Observing the ineffectiveness of military measures against nationalist propaganda as well as the spread of armed rebellion in Kabylia and the northern Constantinois, he attempted to reopen the dialogue with the moderate nationalists without daring to propose a political solution. His initiative was limited to trifling small-scale reforms suggested by his colleagues, such as increasing the number of Muslim civil servants and establishing so-called Social Centres to provide the more impoverished Muslim communities with basic technical assistance. Generally, he concurred with the initiatives of the army. The number of troops was increased by calling up reservists, bringing the total to 120,000 men. In the best nineteenth-century tradition, General Parlange instinctively went back to the idea of the *Bureaux arabes*, and set up their modern equivalent in the form of the Specialised Administrative Sections (SAS). The *Goum* (lit. *qawm*, 'people', 'tribe') native irregulars, who likewise belonged with the old *Armée de l'Afrique*, were reconstituted under the name of Mobile Rural Police Groups or GMPR. This simple return to institutions which had been useful in the past for the administration of conquered tribes was a political mistake, coming as it did at the time of the celebrated Bandung Conference of newly-independent nations in April 1955, and

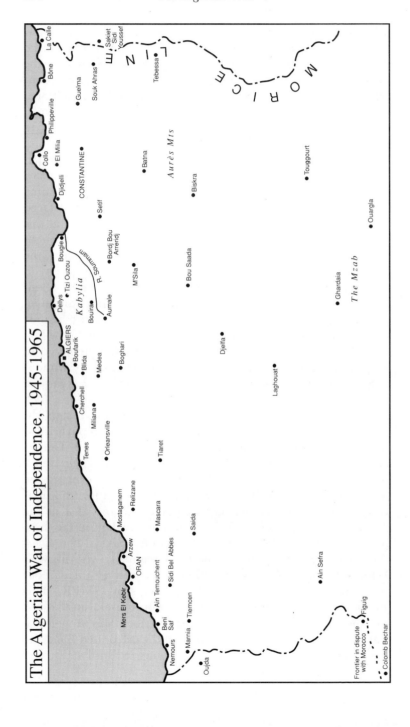

The Algerian War of Independence, 1945–1965

especially when the neighbouring French protectorates of Tunisia and Morocco were moving towards complete independence. Such failure to measure up to the requirements of the situation played into the hands of the Algerian nationalists, who employed Radio Cairo's 'Voice of the Arabs' to gain an audience, and turned to the United Nations, where the Algerian question was first put down for discussion on 30 September 1955. Militarily, they enjoyed the active support of Nasser's Egypt. In Algeria itself, their own political-administrative organisation (OPA) was progressively installed by the FLN in place of local French government. To counter such advances, Soustelle clutched at a belief in the merits of the old policy of assimilation, now renamed 'integration'. This about-turn surprised everyone up to and including the new premier, Edgar Faure, who did not dare make himself responsible for this personal choice by the governor-general, but fell back upon preparations for a 'loyal application' of the 1947 *Statut*.

While France hesitated between various outdated solutions, a dramatic incident revealed the determination of the FLN. On 20 and 21 August 1955 the Front's *wilaya* or province of the Northern Constantinois, assisted by the local Muslim population, unleashed an attack on thirty-six centres of colonisation. This suicidal operation, in which the attackers lost 1,273 of their number against 123 victims of the attack including seventy-one Europeans, provoked the desired split between Muslims and Europeans. In their reprisals, the latter henceforth regarded all Muslims as rebels, while Muslims themselves came to regard the as yet poorly organised bands of the *Armée de Libération Nationale* as *mujāhidin* or fighters in the Holy War. Muslim *élus*, shocked by what was happening, impressed or intimidated by the FLN, resigned; in the Algerian Assembly, even the old official candidates began to speak of 'the Algerian national idea' in the Motion of the Sixty-One, passed by the Muslim representatives of the second college on 26 September 1955.

The intensification of the military conflict was no solution; France could not escape the need for a definite Algerian policy. Faure as prime minister wanted the electorate to give its opinion, and after the dissolution of the National Assembly on

2 December, France tacitly returned its verdict at the general election. The victory of the 'Republican Front' of the left-wingers Guy Mollet and Mendès-France heralded the rejection of the policy of integration and the recognition of 'Algerian identity'. The Europeans of Algeria, on the other hand, immediately demonstrated against the decision of the mother-country. As in 1863 and 1871 they invoked the revolutionary principle of public safety, throwing up defence committees to prove their serious intentions. From the moment of his nomination in place of Soustelle early in 1956, the new governor-general Catroux, who was identified with the Gaullist reforms of 1944, found himself aggressively defied by the Algiers mob, while they gave Soustelle a hero's farewell on his departure for Paris. When Mollet as prime minister arrived in Algiers on 6 February 1956, the Europeans made their feelings only too clear with a furious demonstration, and immediately obtained satisfaction: Catroux was obliged to make way for yet another man, Robert Lacoste. Mollet proceeded to declare in Algiers that 'the bonds between France and Algeria are indissoluble', while stating in Paris that free discussions were to be held with the Muslim *élus*. On 12 March he went on to obtain from the National Assembly, including the Communist deputies, the grant of special powers to re-establish order in Algeria and introduce a policy of democracy. Henceforth the governor-general in Algiers, now elevated to the position of Resident Minister, had dictatorial powers to achieve it.

As between the re-establishment of order and the introduction of democracy, however, priority was given by the new Minister, Lacoste, to the military problem. This resolute former trade unionist and admirer of Bugeaud subordinated everything to his desire to crush Algerian nationalism. At his request the government recalled the national service intake of 1953, then that of 1952, and gave the army greatly extended powers. Now, with a strength of some 400,000 men, it proceeded to the famous *quadrillage* or division of the country into military zones, and began the construction of immense fortified barriers, notably on the border with Tunisia. The next step, the *ratissage* or combing of the new military sectors for guerrillas, was designed to go hand in hand with the resumption of control over the native population. The army was, in effect, invited to build the new Algeria, a commission which soon made it the principal political force in the country.

Little by little, political and administrative problems ceased to be the exclusive concern of the Resident Minister and the government. Whereas at the beginning of 1956 the dissolution of the Algerian Assembly and the abolition of the *communes mixtes* was to have been the occasion for increasing the number of elected Muslim representatives and encouraging the appearance of a 'Third Force' of Muslims opposed to the FLN, such political initiatives rapidly gave way to simple administrative reforms in harmony with military requirements. Thus the number of *départements* was increased and the integration of the vast Saharan territories into the government of Algeria proper was secured despite metropolitan plans for a 'French Sahara'. Local government reform, which for the first time allowed Muslims to direct a *commune*, should have had a stronger political impact, but it coincided with the takeover of responsibility for the Muslim communities by the new Specialised Administrative Sections of the army. And agrarian reform, announced as a revolutionary new policy, was of little practical effect. The new *Statut de l'Algérie*, which was to have been negotiated with the *élus* of Algeria, was devised in accordance with initiatives taken by the army to divide rather than unite the country, the so-called 'Kabyle policy' of playing upon ethnic divisions. When, finally, all elected councils were dissolved on 5 December 1956, 'the new Algeria' projected by the government reverted to the old 'regime of the sword'.

Meanwhile, in the course of 1956 the FLN intensified its military and political activity. In addition to its guerrilla activities, which were extended westwards into the Oranais as well as into the towns, the *Front* scored some notable political successes: the rallying of the *oulema* and the underground Algerian Communist Party; the formation of the trades unions UGTA and UGEMA;[1] the indefinite strike of Muslim students and schoolchildren; and the desertion of Algerians in the armed forces, both officers and other ranks. Most important of all, since April 1956 the moderate nationalist leaders had joined the FLN in Cairo, while Lamine Debbaghine, a former MTLD

[1] The *Union Générale des Travailleurs Algériens* and the *Union Générale des Étudiants Musulmans Algériens*.

man, had become the first president of the new FLN executive; within Algeria support for Messali Hadj had collapsed. Only the beginnings of a rift appeared when the leaders of the FLN inside the country as distinct from outside seemingly decided entirely on their own initiative to hold an important secret congress. This, the Congress of the Soummam in Kabylia, was held on 20 August 1956, a date which allowed no time for the external leadership to be present. Major decisions were nevertheless taken. The National Liberation Army (ALN) was provided with a single general staff under Belkacem Krim. The political leadership of the FLN was entrusted to a National Council of the Algerian Revolution, or CNRA, composed of thirty-four members — elected at the Congress — with a five-member Committee for Coordination and Execution (CCE). The combatants resolved to retain a collective leadership, and laid down the aim of their struggle: a single, democratic and socialist Algerian Republic.

In France, the Congress of the *Section Française de l'Internationale Ouvrière* (SFIO) or French Socialist Party declared itself in favour of a ceasefire and a negotiated solution. Its leader, the prime minister Mollet, arranged contacts with the FLN, but these were broken off at the end of September 1956 after two exploratory meetings in Rome and Belgrade. On 22 October a Moroccan aircraft carrying four of the major external leaders of the FLN — Ben Bella, Bou Diaf, Ait Ahmed and Khider — was intercepted on the orders of Max Lejeune, the Secretary of State for the Armed Forces in charge of Algerian Affairs, and the four men were interned in France. Further negotiations were now impossible. Nevertheless, on 31 October the government proceeded to make matters even worse when it took part in the Anglo-French landings at Suez in conjunction with the Israeli invasion of Egypt, which from the French point of view was designed to strike at the Egyptian base of the FLN. The failure of this adventure and the seizure of the Moroccan aircraft discredited France while greatly increasing the stature of the Arabs in the eyes of the world. In Algeria itself the assurances of Lacoste and Mollet that 'Today pacification is certain; no-one can still believe in the victory of the *fellaghas*', rang hollow. The Muslim population increasingly evaded French authority.

The European population, still without any understanding of the Muslim revolt, reacted ever more angrily. Extremists who preached direct action quickly found wide support. By continually accusing the Socialist government of preparing to abandon Algeria, these 'ultras' created their own climate of revolution. The funeral of Amédée Froger, mayor of Boufarik, a great landowner and political leader of the European right, who was shot by the terrorist Ali la Pointe on 22 December 1956, was their opportunity for violent demonstrations followed by terrorist attacks of their own: bombs were left in Muslim cinemas and in the Casbah, the old Muslim city of Algiers, and a bazooka was fired at the new commander-in-chief, General Salan. After the execution of two convicted ALN guerrillas, the FLN in turn decided upon urban terrorism; Algiers in particular experienced a whole series of murderous incidents. It was then that Lacoste gave the paratroopers the task of destroying the terrorist commandos in the city 'by any means'. The 'Battle of Algiers', lasting from January to September 1957, ended in the destruction of the terrorist organisation in the capital, but psychologically it proved a pyrrhic victory. Treated as helots, the Muslim population of Algiers taught the whole of Muslim Algeria to hate the name 'French'. And French public opinion was equally shocked to hear of the torture of young women, and the torturing to death of a university student, Maurice Audin.

During 1957 there was bitter fighting in the interior with guerrilla units of the Algerian army. Severely damaged, such units were rebuilt with difficulty by the ALN because of the growing scarcity of arms. The round-up and regrouping of the population by the French army contributed still more to their isolation, even though they kept a firm hold on whole regions like Collo, Djidjelli and El Milia. Meanwhile the ALN had to fight its own dissidents in the Aurès and those few guerrillas loyal to Messali Hadj; the massacre of the Messalist *douar* of Melouza simply drove the so-called 'General Bellounis', who held the Djelfa region for a short time against the ALN, into the arms of the French. Thanks to Tunisia, the ALN did at least retain an eastern base, from which it launched its raids with impunity until the fortified Morice line along the frontier was completed. On the political front, the internal leaders of the movement who composed the CCE were forced out of Algiers after the capture and execution of Ben Mhidi, but took refuge in Tunis where they reorganised, this time to the benefit of the external delegation or wing of the Front. Meeting in Cairo, the CNRA raised the membership of the CCE from five to nine; one figure who was brought in was Ferhat Abbas.

The French government, disturbed by the formation of a North African front at the UN, now finally turned its back upon any discussion of the *Statut de l'Algérie* with a representative body of Muslim *élus*, and instead presented to parliament a *loi-cadre* or outline law on 13 September 1957, seven days before the Algerian question was due to be discussed in the United Nations General Assembly. 'Handed down' by France, the law itself, which promised 'respect for Algerian identity' while keeping Algeria 'an integral part of France', was obscure. The purpose behind its proposal to break up Algeria into 'autonomous territories' and *départements*, was apparently to kill Algerian nationalism by playing upon provincialism and ethnic loyalties. 'Divide and rule' certainly seems to have been the motto of its framers, but since it envisaged a single electorate with elections in the near future, it aroused the wrath of the Europeans of Algeria and the anxiety of the French Right. Thrown out by the National Assembly on 30 September, it was amended: *Conseils des Communautés* or assemblies for each community were to be created alongside the future federal institutions, doubling up on the *Conseils des Territoires* (district assemblies). Approved by parliament on 5 February 1958 with more resignation than enthusiasm, the *loi-cadre* allowed for the legal recognition of five such territories, of which one was Kabylia. The FLN described the law as a 'ridiculous attempt to dismember Algeria', and forbade Muslims to stand for the various assemblies it proposed. As Resident Minister, Lacoste had to nominate the councillors in the *communes*, but he did not succeed in getting them to appoint the members of the territorial assemblies before time ran out.

The year 1958 had opened with the French air force bombing of the Tunisian village of Sakiet Sidi Youssef in retaliation for raids by the ALN. The Tunisian government, watching out for just such a blunder, immediately obtained the good offices of the United States and Britain for mediation designed to

internationalise the Algerian problem. The Gaillard government's resigned acceptance of American wishes, which were
made known to the French through Jean Monnet, architect of
France's post-war economic recovery and ultimately of the EC,
contrasted with the assurances of total support given to the
FLN by its sister-nations on the occasion of the Maghrib Unity
Conference at Tangiers. Together they heightened the alarm
at national level in France and among the Europeans of Algeria.
On 26 April these came out onto the streets again in protest,
while the Gaillard government finally fell. Lacoste, certain that
he would no longer be in the new ministerial line-up, declared
that 'we're heading for a diplomatic Dien Bien Phu', and left
Algiers. On 13 May a fresh demonstration provided the pretext
for the occupation of the *gouvernement-general*, the headquarters
of the administration in Algiers, by a small commando of European activists. But on this occasion the Committee of Public
Safety, formed according to the familiar tradition of rioting in
Algiers, was taken over by the army, which demanded the
formation in Paris of a government of Public Safety. General
Salan, the commander-in-chief, gave the name of the man to
lead it as General de Gaulle. To avoid outright civil war, or else
out of scorn for the ephemeral governments of the Fourth
Republic, the French offered no resistance, all expecting that
de Gaulle would put an end to the conflict. But how that was
to be achieved was as obscure as ever. There were those who
hoped for a military victory and others who wanted a negotiated
settlement.

9

FROM '13 MAY' TO THE EVIAN AGREEMENT

The Europeans of Algeria and the military were triumphant; the partisans of integration felt their hour had come. While enthusiastic officers of the army's psychological branch, campaigning for the hearts and minds of the Muslim population, staged demonstrations of so-called 'Franco-Muslim fraternisation', Europeans in general persuaded themselves that the Muslims were giving in. This illusion, shared by many soldiers, brought a whole crop of disappointments and dramas, individual and collective.

Quite apart from that, General de Gaulle himself, officially summoned by President Coty and invested with full powers by the National Assembly, was neither the prisoner of the rioters nor of the colonels in Algiers. He was quick to make this plain. On 4 June he came to proclaim on the Forum of Algiers, the square in front of the *gouvernement-général*, that in the name of France he took note of the conversion of the Europeans to the principle of a single college and a single electorate. Nevertheless he rejected integration as the slogan of his appeal for reconciliation. The FLN responded to the appeal with outright refusal, leaving only Messali Hadj to discover, more subtly, 'openings in the mind of General de Gaulle which might possibly lead to the creation of an Algerian state'. After all the yes-votes cast in the constitutional referendum had been counted, which in Algeria came out at 97 per cent, far too many to have any real meaning, de Gaulle set out to reply to the formation by the FLN of a Provisional Government of the Algerian Republic, the GPRA,[1] by delivering yet another psychological blow. His speech at Constantine on 3 October 1958 aimed to win over the Algerian élite by promising Algeria a political and economic future. In five years, France would give the Muslims 250,000

---

[1] The GPRA, announced in Cairo on 19 September, was a clear attempt by the FLN to wrest the initiative from de Gaulle. Under the presidency of Ferhat Abbas, it established itself at Tunis.

ha., 200,000 houses, 400,000 new jobs, raise their wages to the level of those in metropolitan France and send two-thirds of their children to school. Politically he steered clear of integration, which he knew was unacceptable to the Muslim élite, and spoke instead of association. His offer on 23 October of a 'peace of the brave' went even further, opening the way for negotiations, but the GPRA did not dare to respond. De Gaulle's unfortunate phrase 'the white flag of truce' was taken to mean 'the white flag of surrender', and thereafter the new government in exile refused all contacts.

The army, offended by de Gaulle's rejection of the myths of 13 May, naively thought that the presence in the new National Assembly of a solid block of Muslim deputies standing for *l'Algérie française* or French Algeria would be enough to force his hand. But in Paris after the November elections, the seventy-one Algerian deputies including forty-eight Muslims 'elected by the French army' simply formed a new smoke-screen to conceal the political and military realities of the situation. These were the realities that the new commander-in-chief, General Challe, and his civilian colleague Paul Delouvrier, whose title was changed yet again from Resident Minister to Delegate-general, were commissioned to change. Inside an Algeria which was now tightly closed to the infiltration of arms and guerrillas, Challe undertook the methodical destruction of the *katibas* or detachments of the ALN. Carried out with substantial operational forces, moving steadily across the country from east to west, the *ratissage* ('raking') put an end to the armed potential of the rebellion. The parallel programme of *regroupements* uprooted and relocated 2,157,000 *feilahs*, who were henceforth under the control of various paramilitary bodies, even while they were riddled by nationalist cells. On the economic front, the Constantine Plan took off at great speed; the construction of Delouvrier's 'thousand villages' and the building of new suburbs in the towns were enough to make people forget the delay in job creation and agrarian reform. All in all, the fantastic expenditure by France resulted in a real rise in the standard of living for the 30 per cent of Muslims living in the cities, and for the Europeans. In matters of politics and administration, the number of Muslim servicemen and public employees went up to a point at which there were now more Muslim mayors than

French. 'Dad's Algeria was dead', without a doubt, but the world had yet to be convinced.

The General Assembly of the United Nations, which in 1958 had narrowly rejected a resolution recognising the right of the Algerian people to independence, prepared to pass the resolution in 1959, when there was a risk of the United States vote going against France. In the circumstances, after alerting the army as to his intentions in a tour of the officers' messes, de Gaulle announced on 16 September 1959 that after peace had been restored, Algerians would have a right to self-determination. They would have a choice of three solutions: 'secession', total assimilation and self-government in association with France. His own preference for the third solution was once again made clear: 'government of the Algerians by the Algerians relying on French assistance and closely united with France'. But what was in fact being announced was the end of colonial rule.

Distrustful, the GPRA finally announced on 28 September that it was ready to enter into talks about the conditions for a cease-fire and the guarantees of self-determination, on condition that the unity of the nation and the integrity of its territory, including the Sahara, were acknowledged. This semi-acquiescence made the opening of negotiations possible after the failure of the motion on Algeria at the UN, but the GPRA, divided on the issue, blocked the planned negotiations with a manoeuvre: it nominated as its representatives the four leaders kidnapped in 1956 and now held prisoner on the Île d'Aix in the Bay of Biscay. For their part, the Europeans of Algeria felt betrayed, along with the many officers of the army who were committed to the idea of French Algeria and had become thoroughly politicised. The activists, henceforth led by the café-owner Ortiz and the student leader Susini, the founders of the FNF or National French Front, prepared for another coup. The pretext chosen was the recall of General Massu, who (if an interview published by a German journalist is to be believed) had switched from disobedience within the limits of duty, which was traditionally tolerated in the officer corps, to menacing criticism of the government. On 24 January 1960, armed FNF demonstrators machine-gunned the riot police sent to control them, killing fourteen and injuring sixty-one. Clad in the uniform of the *Unités territoriales* (territorial army), the rioters proceeded to barricade themselves into two symbolic redoubts, a gesture of defiance to force the army to come out against the policies of the President of the Republic. But the army, torn both ways, was finally won over by a new speech to the nation by de Gaulle, and by the condemnation voiced by French public opinion. The 'week of the barricades' ended in the capitulation of the rioters and the flight of Ortiz. This time the Europeans blamed the officer corps in no uncertain terms. The GPRA meanwhile, after its reshuffle at Tripoli earlier in the month, began by suggesting on 27 January that the French government was perhaps no longer an *interlocuteur valable*, a valid partner in negotiations; then, feeling more confident about the government's resolution and authority, called on it to remove all doubts about its intentions.

Once more General de Gaulle set out, as his first priority, to convince the army. In yet another tour of the officers' messes he let it be known that in his opinion the Algerians would opt for 'an Algerian Algeria tied to France'. The formula was repeated in a speech on 14 June aimed at the nationalist leaders in particular. The latter, perhaps worried about the morale of their troops (a fear heightened by the affair of Si Salah, commander of *Wilaya 4*, the Algiers district command of the FLN, who in March 1960 made contact with the French authorities), sent a number of negotiators to France under the leadership of Madame Bou Mendjel. But the Melun talks of 25–29 June 1960 came to an abrupt end, as if both sides had been hoping that they would break down. Their failure led the GPRA to turn to the Communist bloc and especially China, which had recognised it as the legitimate government of Algeria since its formation in September 1958, and to harden its position. From now on it was firmly opposed to the principle of 'Algerian Algeria', making self-determination the prerequisite of any negotiation. On its side, France kept up the military struggle, and tried to put pressure on the GPRA by creating committees of elected Algerian representatives. In a speech on 4 November, de Gaulle refloated the idea of negotiations 'once the fighting had come to an end', but reaffirmed his preference for the 'Algerian Algeria' rejected in advance by the FLN. The GPRA could see in the speech no more than another appeal to the so-called

'Third Force' of moderate Muslim opinion, and made no reply, despite the reference to 'the Algerian Republic which will one day exist'. This same speech, coupled with the announcement of a national referendum on the Algerian policy of the head of state, led in Algiers to dramatic resignations and to a violent reaction from the newly-formed *Front de l'Algérie française* (FAF), which claimed 200,000 Muslim adherents.

To test the strength of this opposition and his own popularity with the Muslims, de Gaulle decided to make a second visit to Algeria in December 1960. His arrival provoked not only the boos and hisses of the Europeans but a fresh explosion on the part of their commandos, whose bombs and street violence were once again designed to draw in the army, and particularly the paratroopers, against the government. It also caused the Muslims to break their silence and take to the streets in counter-demonstrations. At Ain Temouchent and Orléansville crowds of Europeans and Muslims came to blows, while the Casbah of Algiers resounded with cries of 'Power to Abbas!' A mass of Algerian flags appeared on the streets of the capital at the beginning of two days of savage rioting. The paratroopers opened fire at Oran as well as Algiers, leaving some 120 people dead. Nearly all were Muslims; but the soldiers did not join the FAF, and once again the projected revolution came to nothing. Instead, on 8 January 1961, the national referendum went ahead on a deliberately vague question of confidence in the President to prepare for Algerian self-determination, giving de Gaulle a free hand to bring the war to a peaceful conclusion. If the Europeans voted 'No', about 60 per cent of the Muslim population turned out in spite of the GPRA's call for a boycott, making the total of 'Yes' votes into 69.09 per cent of those cast, compared to 75.26 per cent in France. As a result the GPRA dropped all its conditions and on 16 January at last declared itself ready to enter into negotiations. But the talks, scheduled to begin at Évian on 7 April, were delayed by the statement of Joxe, the Minister for Algerian Affairs, that he intended to hold discussions at the same time with Messali Hadj. Then on 11 April, a press conference made clear that what de Gaulle now had in mind was the secession of Algeria and the regrouping of the Europeans. This finally triggered off an army *putsch* on 21 April 1961. A military junta of four of the principal generals who had retired from Algeria during the past few years — Salan, Challe, Zeller and Jouhaud — easily seized power in Algiers with the help of paratroopers and German legionnaires. But the conscripts from France, the navy and the greater part of the air force refused to join them, and the attempt collapsed. Salan, Jouhaud, the paratroop colonels and the deserters from the Foreign Legion went underground, while under their leadership the various European terrorist organisations regrouped into the *Organisation de l'Armée Secrète* (OAS), and made off with quantities of weapons.

The negotiations at Évian, which finally opened on 18 May, proved difficult. Even the proclamation of a truce by France and the release of 6,000 detainees were suspected of being some diplomatic ruse. The talks ran into problems not only over the truce, but over the position of the Europeans in the new Algeria, and above all, over possession of the Sahara. The desert had suddenly become valuable with the discovery of oil and natural gas; the Algerians claimed it as an integral part of Algeria, but had some difficulty in making out their historic rights to this no man's land, annexed by the French at the beginning of the century. Adjourned on 13 June by the French delegation, the conference resumed on 20 July at the nearby Château de Lugrin. But after the nationalist demonstrations of July against a French proposal to partition the country between Europeans and Muslims assured them that the Muslim population was entirely on their side, and especially after the Bizerta affair, in which French and Tunisian forces clashed over the French naval base in northern Tunisia to the detriment of France's international position, the Algerian negotiators felt strong enough to demand the immediate handing over of the Sahara, and adjourned the discussion indefinitely.

The GPRA had in fact to call a meeting of the National Council or CNRA to obtain approval for its conduct of the negotiations. When the Council did meet at Tripoli in August, the hostility of the ALN militants to the so-called 'ornamental urns', the front men of the provisional government who were getting all the publicity in the cities of Algeria, ended in the replacement of Ferhat Abbas by a younger, supposedly more revolutionary man, Ben Khedda. The congress reaffirmed its determination not to give any special guarantee to the

Europeans, and to refuse any kind of association and any inter-
ference in the 'Algerian Sahara'. Meanwhile, it affected to hold
France responsible for the assassinations carried out by the
OAS. For its part, the French government announced that since
it was determined to 'disengage' from Algeria, it would allow
the formation of a provisional Algerian Executive which, with
the aid of a local force, would proceed to the business of self-
determination. At the same time it acknowledged that no future
Algerian government would ever renounce its claim to sovereignty over the Sahara, which amounted to an indication of
the French intention to recognise Algerian sovereignty as such.
After a favourable response from Ben Khedda, the GPRA
entered into secret negotiations conducted by Joxe and the new
GPRA Minister for Foreign Affairs, Saad Dahlab.

But it took the eruption of the OAS during the autumn and
winter of 1961–2; the killing of officers, officials and metropolitan judges; the daily, deadly 'Arab hunts', which killed 256
in a fortnight; and the unofficial plans for the partition of
Algeria, to make the GPRA take up the negotiations seriously.
The revolt of European Algeria put its negotiators in a position
of singular strength; the French army was obliged to evacuate
the countryside to regroup in the towns with a high European
population, and forced to fight on two fronts. French public
opinion, revolted by the terrorism of the OAS on French soil,
demanded immediate peace; the government was obliged to
give up the attempt to establish 'organic cooperation between
the communities'. After a first important meeting between
French and Algerian ministers held at Les Rousses on the
Franco-Swiss border on 11–19 February 1962, the Second
Évian Conference finally resulted in the signing of the necessary
accords and a ceasefire on 18 March 1962.

France agreed to recognise the sovereignty of the Algerian
state over the fifteen *départements* of Algeria and the Sahara.
The Algerians themselves would have to decide by referendum if they wanted Algeria to become an independent state
cooperating with France. The transition to independence would
be handled by a provisional executive nominated by the French
government. The French of Algeria would hold dual nationality
for three years, and would then have to choose either French
or Algerian nationality. Their civil rights were recognised,

their representation was to be in proportion to their number, and there was to be a special regime for Algiers and Oran, where the European population was most heavily concentrated. Equally, they would have their own association and a special court to guarantee their protection. French nationals living as foreigners in the country would have no civic rights, but would enjoy the same guarantees. No individuals were to be deprived of their possessions, interests and established rights without an equitable indemnity fixed in advance. France would keep an army of 80,000 in the country for three years, retain its air force bases in the Sahara for five years, and remain in the naval base at Mers el-Kebir outside Oran for fifteen years. With these assurances provided for the interests of France and individual French citizens, France was committed in exchange to the supply of preferential financial aid to the value of the current aid programmes. Close technical, economic, financial and cultural cooperation was envisaged and mapped out in principle. A Franco-Algerian technical body was meanwhile created to develop the riches of the Saharan subsoil; and Algeria undertook to become part of the franc zone.

The signing of the Évian Accords coincided in Algeria with a final, tragic outburst of European terrorism, whose ringleaders had not even considered what had been agreed on 18 March. Despairing of directly involving the army, the OAS tried by the systematic murder of Algerians to provoke massive reprisals by the FLN, obliging the army to intervene and thus restarting the war. This provocation failed, and resulted only in the storming by the army of the Bab el-Oued, the European quarter at the foot of the Casbah in Algiers. Salan, the underground commander of the OAS, having given the order to 'get the people out on to the streets', the French army was even obliged to fire on European demonstrators in the rue d'Isly in Algiers on 26 March. Salan's fellow-conspirators, Colonels Argoud and Gardes, then tried to win over the *harkis* or Muslim irregulars serving with the army under the command of the *bachagha* Boualem,[2] but in vain. Following the national

---

[2] Systematically recruited from 1957 onwards, the *harkis* came to number about 60,000. A major asset to the French army in its war upon the ALN, they paid dearly in the end for their choice of the wrong side.

referendum on the Évian agreement on 8 April, when 90.7 per
cent of French votes were cast in favour of recognising Algerian
independence, the OAS hit back with a scorched earth campaign in which oil installations were sabotaged along with
French schools, and the University of Algiers was burnt. Then,
in a last act of defiance of a 'decadent and corrupted' France,
the original terrorist Susini, directing the OAS after the arrest
of Salan and his associates, negotiated with the FLN on behalf
of the Organisation, the new Provisional Executive acting as
intermediary. On 17 June the FLN promised him an amnesty
in return for an end to the destruction. But already the OAS
commandos and their chiefs were disappearing, 'called to
another field of operations'. As for the Europeans whom they
had so recklessly compromised, they rejected the Évian guarantees and those of 17 June, and in a wave of panic left the
homeland which had been lost to them through the ineptitude
of their own leaders. The massive exodus of the Europeans,
which turned out to be complete and final, overturned all
the provisions of the Évian Accords and returned Algeria to
indigenous Arabo-Berber people. In the Algerian national
referendum of 1 July 1962 to determine the future of the
country, voters opted for independence by 5,975,581 votes to
16,534. After a hundred and thirty-two years of French rule,
Algeria became an independent Arab state.

So many aspects of this long Algerian tragedy still elude the
historian, who cannot therefore pass a considered judgement
upon these last moments. At least he must reject the simplistic
explanations of partisan minds, and of those in particular who
still do not recognise that they had only themselves to blame.
All clear-sighted observers had been able to measure the growing force of the national ideal among Muslim Algerians. A
history rich in lessons — of the Habsburgs who ceded too little
too late; of the British in Egypt and India who knew how to
withdraw step by step and without war; of the French in the
Middle East and Indo-China, who chose to make war and lose
everything — clearly foretold the future and dictated the broad
lines of policy to be followed. Between the Muslims, won to the
idea of the nation, and the Europeans, opposed to any form of
liberal progress, the role of France could only have been that
of arbiter, assisting at the delivery of the infant nationalism and

ensuring the future growth of an Algerian nation which was truly Franco-Muslim. As Rivarol said of the original French Revolution: 'When you wish to avoid a revolution, you must decide upon it and make it yourself.' Except for the efforts made and the reforms accomplished between 1944 and 1947, however, it has to be recognised that the Fourth Republic failed in this difficult but necessary task. The reversion to colonial rule, for which Naegelen was responsible, and the return to the military regime of the conquest precipitated by Lacoste, explain the failure of the Fourth Republic as far as the Muslims were concerned; on the other side, the surrender of the French Premier Mollet on 6 February 1956 when confronted by the European mob explains the persistence of the European militants in their ambition to impose their will on France.

While it is true that Muslims gave a favourable welcome to the first appeals of General de Gaulle, the entry of the army into politics after 13 May 1958 complicated the matter. By making Algeria the bastion of French rather than Muslim nationalism, not only did it rend the national conscience to no avail, but in its fixation upon the myth of making Algeria French it denied to the Europeans of Algeria the reflexes which might have saved them. Obsessed by the tally of its defeats since 1940, and by the myths it had made for itself in Indo-China, the army preferred to see a conspiracy of world Communism in what was simply a deficiency of French government. The only result of this mistaken diagnosis was to prevent the government from making any serious attempt to create a moderate 'third force' on the nationalist side, and to leave it to deal exclusively with the FLN.

On the other hand, there is no need to speak of a sell-out of French Algeria by one government or another. Whatever regime was in power, France could never have succeeded in making Algeria French by a war waged against Arab nationalism in the age of decolonisation. Those who were truly responsible for the loss of the country were all those who, from 1919 to 1954, obstinately blocked or sabotaged every reform, and after 1958 preached integration as a convenient and hypocritical diversion from the real issue. In other words, the prime responsibility is collectively that of the Europeans of Algeria, people who today blame the various French governments of the past for their failure to break 'the resistance of a few local élus' and impose metropolitan policies. In fact, these Europeans were always unanimous in their hostility to any form of liberal policy towards the Muslim population. The successive delays procured first by their elected representatives and then by the various fronts of colonial Algeria resulted only in the ultimate uprooting of the European population of Algeria.

In a wider historical perspective, beyond the attribution of individual or collective responsibility, the French need to understand that, although they had been conquered, the Muslims of Algeria never gave up the struggle. If a handful of Algerian intellectuals felt an attraction to French civilisation which went so far as to connive at its victory, on the whole the vanquished did not give in, but preserved their own culture through their religion and their traditions. Faithful to their religion and their land, the people in general always refused to become French in any way. 'Keep the *mīm* (the first letter of the word for 'no' in Arabic) and the the *mīm* will keep you.' A hundred times in the history of Algeria, the Muslims repeated this maxim along with what the tribe of the Hachem said to Bugeaud in 1841: 'This land is the land of the Arabs. You are no more than passing guests. Even if you stay here for three hundred years like the Turks, you will still have to leave!'

Part V
INDEPENDENT ALGERIA

After a war waged by a relatively united FLN, or one whose disagreements were of little consequence, Algeria came to independence in the midst of division, narrowly avoiding civil war. Soon after the release of Ben Bella and his fellow-prisoners, the FLN experienced the most serious internal crisis of its short history. The assertive Ben Bella was not in favour of collective leadership, and as a revolutionary he rejected the ideological opportunism of the GPRA. Addressing the CNRA at its meeting at Tripoli in June 1962, he attacked the government team and placed it in the minority. Abandoning the congress, therefore, Ben Khedda as head of the GPRA left for Algiers to confirm the authority of his government in the capital. That government was for him the repository of national sovereignty until it handed over its powers to regularly elected representatives of the people.

However, this went against the desire of the majority of the FLN leaders to impose their own idea of the revolution. According to the FLN's new Programme worked out at Tripoli, the 'Popular Democratic Revolution' was to be led by 'the peasantry, the workers and the revolutionary intellectuals' at the expense of feudalism and the Algerian middle classes, whose 'ideology would make the bed for neo-colonialism'. Algeria had to become a popular democracy founded on collectivism and oriented towards the struggle against imperialism.

The dismissal of Colonel Boumedienne as Chief of Staff by GPRA on 30 June 1962 precipitated the conflict. Boumedienne, the commander of the ALN in exile in Morocco, had risen from 1958 onwards to become commander of the whole of the army in Morocco and Tunisia, in other words the bulk of the new regime's fighting forces; he was thus the power behind any throne. Ben Bella immediately allied himself with the colonel's strongest supporters, the general staff of the army in the west, and set up at Tlemcen a *Bureau politique* (political committee) 'with the task of taking Algeria in hand'. Although he was wildly acclaimed in Algiers, Ben Khedda did not stand out

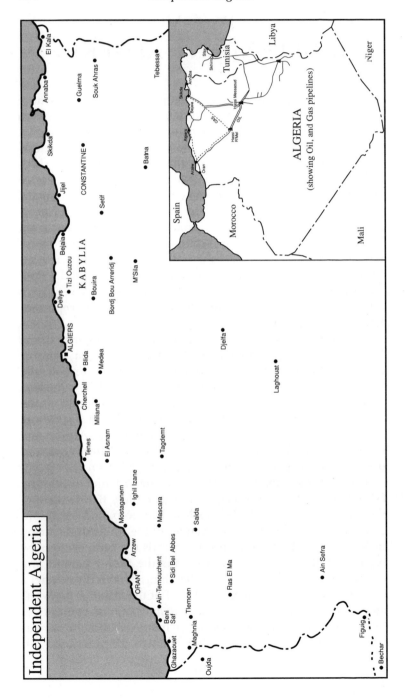

against the formation of this committee, but allowed himself to be drawn into negotiations with it, thus provoking the formation of a third and less conciliatory group by Belkacem Krim and Boudiaf with its headquarters at Tizi Ouzou in Greater Kabylia, which 'called upon the Algerian people in face of the ALN's *coup d'état*'. A compromise was reached on 2 August in favour of an enlarged *Bureau politique*, but this was in fact a victory for Ben Bella. The GPRA faded away.

Meanwhile a period of anarchy prevailed in the absence of clear leadership, which provided an opportunity for the settling of scores. Several thousand *harkis* and pro-French Muslims were executed and many Europeans were abducted: according to official figures, 1,800 of them 'disappeared'. It also brought about a fresh exodus from the country which paralysed both the economy and the administration of the Provisional Executive. Moreover, while the new *Bureau politique* was organising the national election to approve the 196 candidates whom it had selected for the campaign, the internal conflict broke out again between the supporters and opponents of Ben Bella, between civilians and the military, and between the units of the various *wilayas*, the provinces into which the FLN had originally divided the country. Murderous exchanges of gunfire broke out in Algiers itself between supporters of the two sides, while bloody encounters occurred at Boghari, Aumale and Orléansville, among other places, between Boumedienne's *Armée Nationale Populaire* (ANP) and *Wilaya 4*. Appalled at this sport of the new kings, ordinary people demonstrated with the cry of '*Baraka*', 'Seven years is enough!' It came to an end when Mohamed Khider, one of the original nine 'historic chiefs' of the revolution and a fellow-prisoner of Ben Bella during the war, arranged a ceasefire between the *wilayas* on 7 September. Algiers was then demilitarised, which allowed Boumedienne's forces to enter the city unopposed on 10 September 1962, thus ensuring a decisive victory for Ben Bella. On 25 September 1962, the newly-elected Constituent National Assembly proclaimed the birth of the Democratic and Popular Algerian Republic. Then, by a vote of 159 to 1, it approved the Ben Bella government, in which there was no member of the outgoing GPRA. However, five soldiers, including Colonel Boumedienne, occupied the key posts. The new government declared its intention to implement as soon as possible a socialist revolution, an agrarian reform, and a general Algerianisation of personnel.

Inspired above all by Arab nationalism, as preached in Egypt by Colonel Nasser, the Algerian Revolution officially rejected both Marxism and the Communist system. Nevertheless, in spite of certain idiosyncracies, it chose the methods of Communist revolutions and rejected those of democratic socialism. The idea of a single party, which had not clearly emerged at the Tripoli Congress, was imposed step by step. The Algerian Communist Party, the Party of Socialist Revolution formed around Ben Bella's opponent Boudiaf, and then all political organisations were and remained prohibited; instead the FLN became 'the one and only party of progress'. By this was meant not the old but the new party, which was born during the crisis in the summer of 1962. The conference of the FLN which was to have taken place at the beginning of 1963 was not in fact held until April 1964, for the very good reason that the party itself had first to be reconstructed. The position of general secretary was held by Khider until April 1963, but it then passed to Ben Bella.

The harnessing of the trades unions, which hoped to remain independent of the party, proved more difficult to achieve. However, following the First Congress of the UGTA or Algerian General Workers' Union, it came 'under the aegis of the FLN, one of its national organisations' and was obliged to withdraw from the International Confederation of Free Trades Unions. The National Constituent Assembly saw its role rapidly diminish. The Constitution itself had been elaborated outside the Assembly, which provoked the resignation of those, like Ferhat Abbas and Krim, who wanted to make the Assembly an instrument of control over the government. Presidential and authoritarian in character and revolutionary in style, the constitution was accepted by referendum on 8 September 1963, with 5,166,185 votes in favour and 105,047 against. Ben Bella was then elected President of the Republic by 5,865,103 votes.

In 1963, Algerian socialism was principally concerned to identify itself with a peasant revolution. Of peasant origin himself, Ben Bella was naturally inclined to turn his attention to the countryside; he distrusted the continual demands of workers and towns-dwellers. More generally, under the influ-

ence of theorists such as Frantz Fanon, the FLN developed a
myth according to which all revolutions of colonised peoples
were rural in origin. Finally and most important, revolutionary
Algeria had the good fortune to dispose of the lands of colonisation under full cultivation. Lands abandoned by departing
colons were declared 'vacant' and entrusted to *comités de gestion*
(management committees) made up of former agricultural
labourers. Other properties became similarly 'vacant' after the
colons were expelled by intimidation; yet others, most notably
the great estates of big business, were occupied by the military
and nationalised. By 1 October 1963, all land in French possession had been nationalised.

The socialist sector of the economy was thus born from the
reorganisation of former colonial estates and properties into
large agricultural units under *autogestion* or self-management. At
the same time, however, a National Office of Agrarian Reform,
the ONRA, was created, with a heavy state bureaucracy that
stifled the demands of the local committees for autonomy
without breathing any other kind of life into them. The ONRA
was dissolved in 1966 when it became clear that the deficit of
the socialist sector had reached 1,000 million Algerian dinars.[1]
Meanwhile rural self-management, which in 1965 covered
2,302,280 ha. and was responsible for all modern agriculture in
the country, had by 1968 trained only 115,000 permanent
workers out of an active agricultural population of 1,300,000,
even though the management committees — their numbers
were reduced from 3,300 to 1,650 in 1969 — accounted for 60
per cent of the country's gross agricultural product. In industry
and commerce all 'vacant' enterprises were likewise given over
to self-management, as were several important industrial
establishments owned by French companies. A number of
Algerian businesses and properties were similarly entrusted to
management cooperatives. The numbers involved, however,
remained small; self-managed industrial enterprises had a total
of no more than 10,000 workers. Foreign trade was mostly
monopolised by a state-controlled office, the *Office National de
Commercialisation* (ONACO).

This hasty introduction of socialism into a country with few
administrative and technical personnel led to economic and

---

[1] The dinar originally = 1 new franc.

financial difficulties. For a long time the self-managed rural sector absorbed most of the available credit, while its operations made heavy losses. Agricultural production remained static while consumer demand continued to rise. Average cereal production did not exceed 16 or 17 million quintals a year, although the amount required had risen to 24–25 million as the population grew at a rate of 3 per cent a year. There had been 12 million Algerians in 1966; in 1981 there were 19. 8 million. The social situation was even more disturbing. In 1963 Algeria had 2 million unemployed and 2,600,000 people with no means of support — figures which adequately explain the various disturbances caused by poverty in this period without any need to invoke 'foreign provocation'. These included peasant revolts, especially in the Constantinois; the spread of banditry; and sporadic but persistent demonstrations by the urban unemployed. All this occurred even though Ben Bella's government had decided to accept the policy of cooperation with France, which by the end of 1962 appeared irretrievably compromised. Over two years the policy resulted in aid worth 2,680 million new francs, and a whole series of decisions favourable to the economy: the completion of works in progress; the sending of volunteer technicians and *coopérants*, (young teachers choosing to go as an alternative to national service in the army); and the purchase of Algerian wine. Immigration into France, moreover, was allowed to continue much as before, and consequently continued to rise. In the early years of independence, there were some 510,000 Algerians in France earning a total of 1,700 million frs.; the number increased to 884,320 in 1975 and to about a million in 1981.

Despite the extent and importance of this Franco-Algerian cooperation between 1963 and 1970, it was for a long time accepted only grudgingly in Algeria. A corresponding section of French opinion complained about 'wasted generosity', and made its point when the French oil companies were nationalised in 1971: 'Cooperation, costly to France and profitable to Algeria, has been the great failure of the Fifth Republic.' To offset the close commercial dependence on France, which in 1964 meant that French imports from Algeria were worth more than 3,000 million dinars against Algerian imports from France amounting to 2,400 million dinars, Algeria set out to develop economic relations first of all with the various Communist-Socialist states of the period, and later with other capitalist countries. Over the years, the Soviet Union provided loans and technical aid but little trade resulted; effectively Algeria's trade came to rest with the countries of the European Economic Community. By about 1980 these accounted for some 70 per cent of the total, only half of which was represented by France. Trade with the countries of the old Communist world remained at less than 5 per cent of the whole, while that of the United States and other American countries rose to about 10 per cent. The position of France as Algeria's chief trading partner was unshaken down to 1970, but its role decreased following the oil nationalisation crisis in 1971, while new partners such as Italy and Japan emerged, and other established ones such as the United States and West Germany strengthened their connections. Such developments were made possible by the exploitation of Saharan oil and natural gas, which in 1963 was the great economic trump in Algeria's hand, and has since become more than ever its chief economic asset. Until 1970 the government in Algiers stood by the principle of collaboration with a variety of foreign oil companies. However, as early as 1967 oil and gas were worth as much as the export of wine or the remittances of Algerians working in France. By itself, state income from their production and sale provided on average 22 per cent of budgetary revenues before nationalisation in 1971.

Closely related to the adoption of socialism in the early stages of Algerian independence was the cultural policy of the new regime. The intention of the Algerian revolution was finally to re-Arabise an Algeria that had been 'depersonalised by colonialism': 'it is not possible to build socialism without Arabisation.' This determination to Arabise has been most strongly marked, as a result, in the crucial field of education. Nevertheless it has presented a considerable problem. Since bilingualism in French and Arabic is regarded as merely 'circumstantial', Algeria has always refused to associate itself with the official French campaign to promote the use of the French language throughout the former empire, developing instead the use of Arabic by all possible means; but this has been a difficult task because literary Arabic, whether classical or modern, is in effect a foreign language for Algerians. In spite of the real progress made by Arabic as the official language of the country, French-Arabic bilingualism remains a fact of life. Newspapers in Arabic are less numerous and less widely read than those in French, and paradoxically the democratisation of education has increased the number of French-speakers. This bilingualism, far from being a handicap, seems to be rather to Algeria's advantage.

In much the same way, the foreign policy of the Democratic and Popular Republic of Algeria which was admitted to the United Nations on 8 October 1962 was based officially upon its geographical situation but above all upon its ideological position. 'Algeria is an integral part of the Arab Maghrib [the Arab West], the Arab world and Africa'; in accordance with Article 2 of the Constitution, it was committed to positive neutrality and non-alignment. The African part of this vocation has been mainly expressed in support for the movements of liberation in Angola and against apartheid in South Africa. Algeria's adherence to the Organisation of African Unity from the latter's foundation in 1963 brought it great popularity among the governments of black Africa, until these came to fear that Algeria might make itself the champion of every subversive movement on the continent. Arabism, on the other hand, to which Ben Bella laid claim both formally and familiarly with his cry 'We are Arabs, Arabs!', was strengthened by various exchanges and by several significant official visits, including one by President Nasser of Egypt to Algiers. Egyptian military aid to the ANP, the Popular National Army which replaced the ALN, was steady, and increased in moments of crisis when Algeria was at odds with her neighbours in the Maghrib.

Far from making progress towards the unification of the Arab Maghrib, which was envisaged at the Conference of Tangier in 1958, the Maghribi dream remained clouded by a succession of diplomatic and military conflicts. In January 1963 President Bourguiba recalled his ambassador from Algeria in protest at the protection it had given to the plotters of a coup against the Tunisian regime. Much more serious was the conflict which broke out in October 1963 between Algiers and Rabat. Since 1960 the Moroccans had hoped for the Saharan frontier between the two countries, which had been established at their expense by France, to be redrawn in their favour under an agreement signed by King Mohammed V with the GPRA. While negotiations were in progress at Oujda, skirmishes took place on the border, and on 8 October Algerian troops seized a number of positions, which were then reoccupied by the Moroccans on 14 October. Algeria ordered a general mobilisation of the former *djounoud* (soldiers of the ALN),[2] and denounced the new Moroccan King, Hassan II, as 'a puppet king, a criminal'. The mediation of Emperor Haile Sellassie of Ethiopia resulted in the Bamako Conference and the acceptance of a ceasefire on the basis of the *status quo*. The conflict, however, did not go away, and resumed in the 1970s in the form of support given by Algeria to the Polisario movement in the Western Sahara in its fight against Morocco's annexation of the former Spanish Saharan territories. Although the war in the Sahara died down somewhat in the latter part of the 1980s, the dispute continued to affect relations between the two countries, even when the question of Maghribi unity at last returned to the top of the political agenda in 1988 with proposals for a form of economic union to strengthen North Africa in its relations with the EC.

The conflict with Morocco in 1963 generated a blaze of patriotism which favoured the government in face of the defiance of Ait Ahmed, one of those captured and imprisoned with Ben Bella in 1956, but who had joined the Tizi Ouzou group in 1962, and had since emerged as leader of the opposition in Kabylia. His FFS or Socialist Forces' Front attracted little popular support. However, at a time when the new republic had yet to create a working administration and a viable economy, ideological conflict caused such tasks to be neglected. At the Congress of the FLN in April 1964, the proponents of the Leninist line had their doctrines approved by the party and named their ideological enemies: the *ouléma*, who were regarded as obscurantist; the new class of state officials, who were denounced as an administrative bourgeoisie; and finally the ANP, the only organised force in the country. This virtual declaration of war acted as a fatal provocation to the threatened groups. While Ben Bella hedged, giving pledges first to the

---

[2] Arabic *jundī*, pl. *junūd*.

army and then to the Marxists, and looked for support abroad, the strength of the opposition grew. It accused him of sacrificing Algerian interests to his internationalist revolutionary strategy, and of leading the country to economic ruin and foreign dependence with a socialism more imaginary than effective. As soon as the army had completed the defeat of the FFS in Kabylia, its leader Boumedienne made his move. On 19 June 1965, on the eve of the Afro-Asian Conference in Algiers which was to have made him the hero of the developing world, Ben Bella was arrested, and his friends were powerless to resist. A few of them were imprisoned, while 1,500 of the former regime's political prisoners were freed.

Renouncing all revolutionary romanticism, the government of Boumedienne announced its intention of restoring order in the country and giving it a modern economy. And indeed, in the thirteen years of his government, the new team proved realistic and effective. Politically it surmounted all internal crises, including an abortive coup, and succeeded in the creation of a centralised state. Local and regional institutions were put in place, notably with the reform of the *communes* in 1967 and that of the *wilayas* or administrative districts in 1969. These provided the country with representative institutions: popular communal assemblies at the lowest level, and at the level of the *wilaya*, assemblies elected from lists drawn up by the Party. In 1976 the *Charte nationale* (National Charter) was approved by referendum after popular discussions and consultations, defining the features and ambitions of the socialist state.

On the financial side, thanks to more or less balanced budgets, independence was assured. Surpluses in the working budgets of the various ministries paid for much of the necessary investment in the economic infrastructure of the country, which was otherwise financed by foreign loans. To finance the first Four-Year Plan of 1970–3, however, the government decided upon the move which so affected relations with France, the nationalisation of the petroleum industry at the beginning of 1971. Economically the results were undeniable, as the strong growth in gross domestic product revealed. The motor was industrialisation, which gave rise to a vast industrial state sector created thanks to oil and natural gas, but also to massive investments and foreign aid. Large modern industrial complexes appeared at Skikda, Annaba (formerly Bône) and Arzew, with others provided for under the Second Four-Year Plan of 1974–7. Algeria now has, therefore, a huge iron and steel complex in El Hadjar at Annaba, whose production rose to about 400,000 tonnes of steel in 1977 and almost 900,000 in 1983, approaching the 'magic figure' of 1 million, where it has remained.[3] Likewise it has two oil refineries; plants for fertilisers and the liquefaction of natural gas; and an important textile complex.

Rapid progress was also achieved in education and professional training, making possible a progressive Algerianisation of managerial and technical personnel. In 1963, Algeria had 1,039,000 children in primary and secondary education, a figure which had risen to about 5 million in 1984, while in higher education the figure went up from 2,800 in 1963 to 79,000 in 1980 and 96,000 in 1982, creating a student body of more than 100,000 today. All independent, Catholic schools outside the old French state system were incorporated into the new single Algerian system, which is specifically Muslim; the number of mosques has roughly trebled to over 6,000.

The underlying purpose of the First and especially the Second Four-Year Plan, however, was to accelerate the process of industrialisation until the whole of the economy 'took off' into self-sustaining growth. Algeria certainly benefited from a substantial increase in dollar income in 1976 with the rise in the price of natural gas and oil, production of which reached 50 million tonnes. Moreover, the new heavy industries brought a great increase in the number of non-agricultural jobs, which quadrupled in the twenty years 1965–85.[4] Half the adults in the towns and semi-urban agglomerations now have some permanent professional employment. 'Take-off', on the other hand, has been hindered from the start by the world crisis which began in 1973, by the slowing down of remittances from

[3] Figures from United Nations Economic Commission for Africa, *African Statistical Yearbook*, 1986, Part 1, *North Africa*. Despite the increase, they have continued to fall well short of the capacity of the plant, a reflection on the overall success of the programme; cf. Mahfoud Bennoune, *The Making of Contemporary Algeria, 1830–1987*, Cambridge, 1988, and Ali El Kenz, *Le complèxe sidérurgique d'El Hadjar. Une expérience industrielle en Algèrie*, Paris, 1987.
[4] UNECA, *African Statistical Handbook*, 1986.

Algerians working abroad, and by a subsequent decline in oil exports. Algeria has been obliged in consequence to increase its foreign debt to the point at which repayments have been running at 16–17 per cent of the value of exports. Even more serious, because more fundamental, is the fact that in the rural areas, employment has remained stagnant, and has indeed declined, while unemployment has continued to increase in a countryside deprived of resources; agriculture, which in 1966 employed more than half the working population, accounted for no more than a quarter by 1985.[5] Agricultural production has equally failed to grow, and is now far outstripped by demand.

The ambitious agrarian reform which was introduced in 1971 to accompany the programme of industrialisation was applied to 1,141,000 ha. of cultivable land over the next three years, 1972–5. It was based upon a system of cooperatives, of which 5,980 were eventually created between 1972 and 1980.[6] These were of three different types, with an average area of 180 ha., involving some 110,000 peasants as compared to roughly 230,000 in the state sector of lands under *autogestion*. But the nationalisation of lands whose owners were not themselves farmers or who were simply absentees, together with the limitation placed upon the size of the larger private properties, was carried out very cautiously, so that in the end little more than 10 per cent of land in private ownership was taken over by the state for reallocation. Agrarian reform as a result caused few upheavals, and generated little enthusiasm among its beneficiaries, about 8 per cent of whom in fact gave up. It was inevitable that the involvement of over 7 million peasants in a transformation of this magnitude, dictated by the government and subordinated to the policy of industrialisation, would be a lengthy process. Lack of determination ensured its failure. In 1984 the reform was finally abandoned, after 450,000 ha. had been redistributed to individual farmers.[7]

[5] Bennoune, *Making of Contemporary Algeria*, 253,287, and M. Ollivier, 'L'économie algérienne vingt ans après 1966: l'indépendance nationale en question', *Annuaire de l'Afrique du Nord*, XXIV (1985), 417-57, an excellent analysis of Algeria's problems.
[6] Cf. Bennoune, *Making of Contemporary Algeria*, 190-3.
[7] K. Pfeifer, *Agrarian Reform under State Capitalism in Algeria*, Boulder, 1985.

These and other social and economic problems came to the fore after the death of Boumedienne on 27 December 1978, and the election of President Chedli Boudjedid as his successor on 7 February 1979. The new government had to confront a whole series of problems arising mostly from rapid growth of the population, which had virtually doubled since indepen- / dence, together with even more rapid urbanisation, which had doubled the size of the towns and cities over the previous ten years. The difficulties presented by this huge increase were compounded by the priority given to the supposedly 'industrialising' industries created by the four-year plans, those which were intended to stimulate the sectors more directly related to consumer demand. The housing situation was catastrophic; a million new apartments were required over the next ten years just to keep the shortfall at the same level. In the same way, the flagrant inadequacy of the water supply system was giving rise to water rationing in the majority of towns. The exodus from the countryside called urgently for measures to improve the standard of rural life and for incentives to increase the level of agricultural production.

Politically, it became clear that public opinion was in favour of a certain liberalisation of the regime. At the same time, however, political and social tensions were coming into the open between the mutually opposed Marxist, reformist and conservative tendencies; between the new generation of those who had come up through the 'Arab mill' of the education system and students who were still French-speaking; between workers in the towns and workers in the countryside; and between the cities of the north and the deprived south, where the chief natural resources of the country nevertheless lie. The party and the president were called upon to hold a delicate balance, a task made more difficult by the fact that the legitimacy of the party in a one-party state is often more dependent on popular confidence than on ideological purity. They were not helped by the 'Berber Spring' of March 1980, violent protests which erupted in the Berber homeland of Kabylia against the policy of Arabisation, raising the spectre of ethnic unrest in a region noted for its opposition to Ben Bella.

Accordingly, on 5 July 1982 Algeria celebrated the twentieth anniversary of its independence with some circumspection. To rebuild its internal market and attain economic independence — the object of its three successive plans — the country had become extensively industrialised. To make the necessary investments, it had mobilised its most obvious resource in the form of oil and natural gas, but this assignment of income was inevitably at the expense of other sectors, particularly agriculture, and of the infrastructures of society: housing, transport and other social and cultural amenities. As production frequently failed to reach the planned level, and the industrial machine was running at less than its full capacity, the aim now was to improve both management and productivity, and to revive the sectors previously sacrificed to industrialisation. The 1980–4 Five-Year Plan was conceived partly with this aim in view, its special purpose being to introduce 'a social decade', for which the FLN adopted the motto 'For a better life'. But the question remained whether the exuberant demography of the past twenty years would allow any such thing. Even with a tardy recourse to family planning and birth control, Algeria will see its population double again by the year 2000.

In the following years, in fact, Algeria was simultaneously confronted by the growing need for imports of food and the dramatic decrease in its revenues from oil and gas, its only source of foreign exchange since the demise of colonial agriculture. To deal with this permanent crisis, the state sought to increase agricultural production by restructuring the agricultural sector and doing away with price controls. In the same way it liberalised its general economic policy, encouraging the private sector in industry and allowing foreign investment. As a sign of the transformation, the Planning Ministry was abolished in 1987 and the Chambers of Commerce reopened. But foreign debts amounted to US$21 billion, and the country was weighed down by repayments of capital and interest.

In the circumstances, the remedies proposed by the regime were not only long overdue and much too late; they appeared either trivial or ineffective to a population exasperated by growing unemployment (1,200,000 was the official figure), endless shortages, the rising cost of living and the freezing of wages. All classes now look for change, not always reckoning with the inescapable facts of the country's economy and demography. The predominance of youth in a population of which 75 per cent are under twenty-five years of age has made the nation especially ready to respond to Muslim preachers who deliver a message of justice and equality and denounce the corruption of the state. All these factors help to explain the spontaneous disturbances which shook Algiers and other cities from 5 to 12 October 1988. They were basically bread riots, for food and housing, but they expressed an equally fervent longing for liberty and democracy. The National People's Army repressed them with quite unnecessary bloodshed, leaving between 200 and 500 people dead, according to the various sources, and several hundreds wounded.

The outlawed political opposition seized the opportunity to declare that the riots were 'the consequence of twenty-six years of dictatorship and one-party government which has led Algeria into bankruptcy — economic, social and political'. The FLN itself gave as the causes the collapse in petrol prices which 'for three years has deprived Algeria of half its overseas earnings', and the policy of austerity which this had entailed, unpopular but necessary. Whatever the reason, the rejection of the party by the people was unmistakable. President Chedli, first promising the liberalisation of the regime, then bringing in constitutional reform, had apparently regained the confidence of his people when the proposal to amend the constitution was approved by referendum in November with 92 per cent in favour, and when he himself was re-elected on 22 December for a five-year term of office with 81 per cent of votes cast, admittedly as the only candidate. In the same way the new constitution, bringing in a somewhat more democratic regime, was approved by a second referendum in March 1989 with 73 per cent voting 'yes'; and the FLN too believed the crisis to be past.

The moment of truth, however, came with the municipal and departmental elections in June 1990. These were the first free elections, open to 136,000 candidates from eleven parties, that Algeria had known since 1962. In spite of the low turnout, with abstentions amounting to 35 per cent of the electorate, they produced a landslide for the Islamists. The *Front islamique du salut* (FIS), the Islamic Salvation Front, a party hastily put together in 1989, polled some 65 per cent of the votes cast, and won in forty-five out of the forty-eight *wilayas*. This punishing protest vote came as a shock to the government, which talked of 'a collection of malcontents'; and certainly the significance of this unexpected infatuation with a party which lacked a political programme, preaching only a return to Islam as 'guardian of the authenticity and identity of the Algerian nation', was by no means clear. Was it, for example, a temporary disappointment with the promise of socialism, or an unequivocal condemnation of the single-party state? Or did it rather mean that the majority of Algerians, balloted on the choice between the Arab world and Europe, had definitely rejected all forms of foreign materialism, preferring in their place the moral order of traditionalism, and a theocratic state according to Islamic law? The answer lies in the future, but a future which at the time of writing is very close, for the expected parliamentary elections are to be held early in 1991. The result of those elections may depend upon the mobilisation of democratic forces within the country, and their union with the movement of Berber nationalism, which has flourished again ever since the 'Berber Spring' of 1980. It will most certainly depend upon the attitude of the army, which ever since the *coup d'état* which removed Ben Bella on 19 June 1965 has been the true ruler of Algeria.

BIBLIOGRAPHY

BY MICHAEL BRETT

Charles-Robert Ageron's short *Histoire de l'Algérie contemporaine*, here translated as *A History of Modern Algeria*, is a masterpiece of historical writing which sets out its subject clearly, completely, and economically, and remains the best and most balanced account of the whole of the period from the French conquest in 1830 to the present day. First published in 1964, it announced an impressive series of works by the author, including the magisterial *Les Algériens musulmans et la France, 1870-1919*, and the second volume of a much larger *Histoire de l'Algérie contemporaine*: Vol. II, *1871-1954*. These two books, together with the large collection of shorter studies partially listed here under Authors and Titles, give solid support for the *History of Modern Algeria*, and are an endless source of further information. Ch.-A. Julien's *Histoire de l'Algérie contemporaine*, Vol. I, *Conquête et colonisation*, goes together with the work of Ageron for the period 1827-70; Vol. III has not yet appeared.

The history of Algeria contained in this *corpus* must nevertheless be seen in at least two contexts: that of France and the French empire, and that of North Africa and the Middle East. For the history of France there is no better introduction for the English-speaking reader than Alfred Cobban, *A History of Modern France*, Vol. II, *1799-1871*; Vol. III, *1871-1962*. Reading about the French overseas empire might begin with Henri Brunschwig, *French Colonialism, 1871-1914*, and continue with ✴ S. Roberts, *History of French Colonial Policy, 1870-1925*; James J. Cooke, *New French Imperialism, 1880-1910*; and Andrew and Kanya-Forstner, *France Overseas: the Great War and the Climax of French Imperial Expansion*; in French, H. Blet, *Histoire de la colonisation française*; H. Deschamps, *Méthodes et doctrines coloniales de la France du XVIe siècle à nos jours*; and G. Hardy, *Histoire sociale de la colonisation française*. Ageron himself, however, is currently engaged upon a *Histoire de la France coloniale*, of which Vol. II, *La décolonisation*, has appeared.

The literature on Algeria in the context of North Africa is

146   *Bibliography*

usefully discussed in four review articles in the *Journal of African History*: Douglas Johnson, 'Algeria: some problems of modern history' (1964); and Michael Brett, 'Problems in the interpretation of the history of the Maghrib' (1972); —, 'The colonial period in the Maghrib and its aftermath' (1976); —, 'Continuity and change: Egypt and North Africa in the nineteenth century' (1986). The literature itself must begin with J.M. Abun-Nasr, *A History of the Maghrib in the Islamic Period*, the only modern history of the whole subject, including Libya. Ch.-A. Julien's epoch-making *Histoire de l'Afrique du Nord* of 1931 has not been updated for the colonial period; the critical third volume of the second edition has never appeared. The English translation of the second volume, *History of North Africa from the Arab Conquest to 1830*, is nevertheless a good introduction to the subject. A substantial collective history of the nineteenth and twentieth centuries is to be found in Vols V–VIII of *The Cambridge History of Africa*, set in the context of the continent as a whole; eventually, this will also be true of the *UNESCO General History of Africa*. The excellent analysis by Elbaki Hermassi, *Leadership and National Development in North Africa*, systematically compares and contrasts the histories of Algeria, Tunisia and Morocco to explain the differences between their post-colonial regimes; the emphasis upon their past and present differences is a useful corrective to interpretations in more general terms of colonialism and imperialism.

Within this broad category, Lucette Valensi, *On the Eve of Colonialism. North Africa before the French Conquest, 1790–1830*, gives a pessimistic view of the early nineteenth century; Magali Morsy, *North Africa 1800–1900*, one still more pessimistic of the century as a whole. In the twentieth century, when the politics of resistance to conquest gave way to the politics of movements for independence, the rise of nationalism is vigorously celebrated by Ch.-A. Julien in his polemical attack on French policies in 1952, *L'Afrique du Nord en marche* (whose third edition is provided with an equally argumentative bibliographical essay), and drily described from a conservative point of view by Roger Le Tourneau, *Evolution politique de l'Afrique du Nord musulmane*. The long reflection upon the conflict between immigrant European and indigenous Muslim society by Jacques Berque, *French North Africa: the Maghreb between two*

World Wars, develops the theme of a crisis of capitalism in the inter-war period underlying the rise of nationalism at the expense of colonialism. Difficult but rewarding, it takes up the theory of colonial mentalities propounded by Albert Memmi, *The Colonizer and the Colonized*, and applied to the Algerian war by Frantz Fanon in *A Dying Colonialism*. Fanon's position as a theorist of the Algerian war and of anti-colonial revolution in general makes his writing important, especially since his ideas have influenced a generation of North African historians anxious to 'decolonise' their history by showing how it has been systematically deformed by colonial writers for colonial purposes. This revaluation of the past, described by John Wansbrough in 'The decolonization of North African history', *J. African History* (1967), is best seen in A. Laroui, *History of the Maghreb*, while a good example of the target is Eugène Guernier, *La Berberie, l'Islam et la France*.

Two descriptive works of considerable historical value are Nevill Barbour, ed., *A Survey of North West Africa (The Maghrib)*, 1959, and its third edition by Wilfrid Knapp, *North West Africa: A Political and Economic Survey*, 1977. The successive editions of Jean Despois' geography, *L'Afrique du Nord*, 1949, 1958 and 1964, followed by Despois and Raynal, *Géographie de l'Afrique du Nord-Ouest*, are similarly useful. Economic history, fundamental to Ageron's story, is dealt with comparatively by Charles Issawi, *An Economic History of the Middle East and North Africa*, and by Samir Amin, *The Maghreb in the Modern World*; R. Gallissot, *L'économie de l'Afrique du Nord*, and A. Tiano, *Le Maghreb entre les mythes*, and *Le développement économique du Maghreb*, look at the results and prospects in the aftermath of independence. Clarke and Fisher, *Populations of the Middle East and North Africa*, provide individual essays on individual countries. The *Annuaire de l'Afrique du Nord*, beginning in 1962, not only covers in detail the events of the years since Algerian independence, but offers major thematic studies of the region in all its aspects, as well as a comprehensive bibliography of everything published on the subject since its foundation.

Richard I. Lawless, *Algeria*, is an introductory bibliography; his *Algerian Bibliography: English Language Publications, 1830–1973* is most useful, though incomplete, especially since it lists the extensive, and informative, travel literature which proliferated from the 1860s onwards, when Algiers first became a tourist resort. So too is the English-language bibliography in Alf A. Heggoy, *Historical Dictionary of Algeria*. Publications in French and English down to the end of the nineteenth century are exhaustively listed in R.L. Playfair, 'A Bibliography of Algeria' and 'Supplement to the Bibliography of Algeria', reprinted in his *Bibliography of the Barbary States*. Substantial biographies of major Muslim Algerian figures of the period will be found in Ch.-A. Julien *et al.*, eds., *Les Africains*, shorter notices of many more Algerians and French in the various volumes of *Hommes et Destins*, notably Vol. VII, *Maghreb Machrek*. Histories of the country go back to the time of the conquest, but readers might begin with Gsell, Marcais and Yver, *Histoire d'Algérie*, in 1927. All in their different ways are polemical, shots in the battle for Algeria's controversial past, in which Ageron himself is fully engaged: cf. the exchange with Xavier Yacono in *Revue historique* (1970), 121–34, 355–65. Jean-Claude Vatin, *L'Algérie politique. Histoire et société*, discusses the problem and the literature while concentrating, like Hermassi, upon the growth to national independence; see also Lucas and Vatin, *L'Algérie des anthropologues*. Meanwhile Lacoste, Nouschi and Prenant, *L'Algérie, passé et présent*, and M. Lacheraf, *L'Algérie, nation et société*, offer revisionist interpretations of Algerian history in the manner described by Wansbrough as 'transvaluation of past deficiencies'. Claude Martin, *Histoire de l'Algérie française*, defiantly reaffirms the old valuations and views of the colonial period as *l'Algérie heureuse* or 'fortunate Algeria', in contrast to Ferhat Abbas, *La nuit coloniale* or 'colonial night': see below.

√   A useful little account of the much-maligned Turkish period in Algeria is William Spencer, *Algiers in the Age of the Corsairs*; see also R. Gallissot, 'Precolonial Algeria'. The *Revue d'Histoire Maghrébine*, edited by A. Temimi, has done much over the 1970s and 1980s to rescue this particular period from neglect. Temimi himself has studied the eastern region of Algeria in *Le Beylik de Constantine et Hadj Ahmed Bey (1830–1837)*, while Ralph Danziger, *Abd al-Qadir and the Algerians*, discusses the career of the national hero; a second good study is by B.G. Martin, 'Opposition to French colonialism in Algeria: 'Abd al-Qadir, his predecessors and rivals'. Julien, *Histoire de l'Algérie contemporaine*, Vol. I, with its excellent bibliography, gives the whole story of the conquest and occupation down to the rising of Mokrani; Annie Rey-Goldzeiguer, *Le royaume arabe*, is an exhaustive study of the policies of Napoleon III. Ageron's views of *his* hero, the Emperor, are set out in his 'Evolution politique de l'Algérie sous le Second Empire', in *Politiques coloniales au Maghreb*. A.T. Sullivan, *Thomas-Robert Bugeaud*, is a biography; Kenneth J. Perkins, *Qaids, Captains and Colons*, discusses the military administration and its eventual elimination from Algeria north of the Sahara; the compensation found by the army in the conquest of the desert is described by Douglas Porch, *The Conquest of the Sahara*; see also Peter von Sivers, 'Alms and arms: The combative saintliness of the Awlad Sidi Shaykh'. Colonisation is touched on by J. Ruedy, *Land Policy in Colonial Algeria*. Turning to the establishment of civil rule, Brett, 'Legislating for inequality in Algeria', explains how the French came to define the Muslim Algerians as second-class citizens, a major step towards the constitution of colonial Algeria.

Colonial Algeria in its heyday from 1871 to 1940 is Ageron's particular subject. *Les Algériens musulmans et la France* is a minutely documented work whose references compensate to some extent for the absence of notes and bibliography from Vol. II of the large *Histoire de l'Algérie contemporaine*, which the author regrets. Basic information on the country by the end of this period is provided by A. Bernard, *L'Algérie*; by the two volumes of the *Encyclopédie coloniale et maritime. Algérie et Sahara*; and by those of the British Admiralty (Naval Intelligence Division), *Algeria*; its economic history is discussed by A. Benachenhou, *Formation du sous-developpement en Algérie*. Pierre Bourdieu, *The Algerians*, originally in the same series (*Que sais-je?*) as Ageron's short *Histoire*, is an excellent companion to it on the subject of the Muslim population. The impoverishment of this population is described by Andre Nouschi, *Enquête sur le niveau de vie des populations rurales Constantinoises*, while its struggles to adapt are revealed by Jean-Paul Charnay, *La vie musulmane en Algérie*. Charnay's work is based on court cases; and the fundamental importance of the legal system to the position of Muslims is underlined not only by Brett, 'Legislating for inequality', but by David Powers, 'Orientalism, colonialism and legal history'. Allan Christelow, *Muslim Law Courts and the French Colonial State in Algeria*, and 'Algerian Islam in a time of transition', looks at the efforts made by Muslims to reach a political settlement with the French on the basis of 'apartheid', as does von Sivers, 'Insurrection and accommodation'; 'Algerian landownership and rural leadership'; and 'Indigenous administrators in Algeria'. Christelow in particular touches on the unfashionable history of the European population, addressed by David Prochaska in *Making Algeria French*. Marc Baroli, *La vie quotidienne des français en Algérie, 1830–1914*, is a social study of this population; Cooke, 'Eugène Etienne', and 'The colonial origins of colon and Muslim nationalism', examines its political aspect before the First World War. R.D. Lee, 'Regional politics in a unitary system: Colonial Algeria', and M.L. Richardson, 'French Algeria between the wars', are theses available as microfilm reprints which look at European politics between the world wars, as does Mahfoud Kaddache, *La vie politique à Alger de 1919 à 1939*.

Against this background, C.V. Confer, *France and Algeria: The problem of civil and political reform*, examines the beginnings of the nationalist movement in the demand for assimilation, and G. Meynier, *L'Algérie révélée. La guerre de 1914–1918*, the critical episode of the First World War. Nouschi, *La naissance du nationalisme algérien*, and Kaddache, *Histoire du nationalisme algérien*, deal with the rise of nationalism in the interwar period. Ali Merad, *Le reformisme musulman en Algerie*, studies the contribution of Ben Badis and his colleagues: see also *Encyclopaedia of Islam*, 2nd edn, s.v. Iṣlaḥ; yet another thesis in microfilm reprint, J.D. Zagoria, 'The rise and fall of the movement of Messali Hadj', follows the fortunes of the Etoile and the PPA. E. Sivan, *Communisme et nationalisme en Algérie*, describes the failure of Communism to identify itself with Algerian nationalism until the war of independence was in progress. Ageron's studies in *Politiques coloniales au Maghreb* and elsewhere emphasise the importance of the close metropolitan connection in determining the form and the course of nationalist agitation: cf. Brett, 'The Maghrib', in *Cambridge History of Africa*, Vol. VII.

Most of these histories of nationalism, including Benjamin Stora, *Dictionnaire biographique de militants nationalistes algériens*, and *Messali Hadj*, take the story down to 1954. Y.M. Danan, *La vie politique à Alger de 1940 à 1944*, deals with the Second World War, as does James J. Dougherty, *The Politics of Wartime*

Aid, and Khenouf and Brett, 'Algerian nationalism and Allied military strategy'. On the basis of a new collection of documents in course of publication by the Service Historique de l'Armee de la Terre, *La guerre d'Algérie par les documents*, Vol. I, *L'avertissement 1943-1946*, Anthony Clayton has produced a study of the climax at Setif in 1945, 'Cruelty and terror: the case of the May 1945 Setif uprising'. Robert Aron *et al.*, *Les origines de la guerre d'Algérie*, also deals with Setif, and more importantly with the subsequent period to 1954, largely neglected apart from the politics of nationalism. Bourdieu *et al.*, *Travail et travailleurs* ✓ *en Algérie*, is a thorough investigation of the population in the 1950s, part of the mass of government or government-sponsored inquiry into the state of the country provoked in large measure by the war. Ferhat Abbas, *Guerre et révolution d'Algérie*, Vol. I, *La nuit coloniale*, is the retrospective view of the whole subject down to the outbreak of the war of independence by one of the principal actors.

The war itself generated a vast literature. Brett, 'Les écrits anglais sur la guerre de libération algérienne/Writing in English about the Algerian war of liberation', surveys (in English) the writing in English; but the English-language reader should certainly begin with Alastair Horne, *A Savage War of Peace*, ☞ which supplies most of the references in English and French. An exception is Elie Kedourie, 'The retreat from Algeria', a sharp attack upon the view that the war was justified, in line, for example, with Martin: see above. The question, as Ageron makes clear, is central to all subsequent writing about Algerian history; and if the answer today is usually 'yes', it is more often than not qualified by controversy over terrorism, and especially over the splits within the FLN immediately after the war, summed up in the title of Arslan Humbaraci, *Algeria: A Revolution that Failed*. The immense interest aroused by the revolution meant that the new government was immediately subjected (perhaps unfairly) to intense scrutiny by observers of all disciplines and persuasions, generating a literature in which the war itself became an introduction to the problems of independence: cf. notably David C. Gordon, *The Passing of French Algeria*, and William B. Quandt, *Revolution and Political Leadership: Algeria, 1954-1968*, but also, e.g., Zartmann, Ottaway, Clegg, Jackson. Clegg's Marxist interpretation should be compared with

Marnia Lazreg, *The Emergence of Classes in Algeria*. Meanwhile the controversy, apparently laid to rest in Algeria itself by the victory of Boumedienne, has revived in Algeria since his death, producing a notable attack upon the present regime by Mahfoud Bennoune, *The Making of Contemporary Algeria*, largely an examination of economic policies and their justification since independence, which condemns the failures of central planning, but still more the attempt at *perestroika*.

The death of Boumedienne in 1978 began a process of what has now become far-reaching change. It is therefore necessary to distinguish between studies of Algerian politics published before that date, works such as Jean Leca, *L'Algérie politique*, and Bruno Etienne, *L'Algérie. Cultures et révolution*, and those published in the 1980s, notably J. P. Entelis, *Algeria, the Revolution Institutionalized*, Rachid Tlemcani, *State and Revolution in Algeria*, and very usefully, Bernard Cubertafond, *L'Algérie contemporaine*, a second companion to the present work in the *Que sais-je?* series. A similar questioning note has appeared in discussions of cultural issues. The views of Ahmed Taleb Ibrahimi, *De la décolonisation à la revolution culturelle*, broadly expressed the consensus of the 1960s and '70s, despite continuing controversy. But social discontent has revived the Kabyle question, which queries the policy of Arabisation: cf. Hugh Roberts, 'The Kabyle question in contemporary Algeria', and more importantly perhaps, the question of Islam and its relationship to the state: cf. Vatin, 'Religious resistance and state power in Algeria', and 'Popular puritanism versus state reformism'. Women's rights, discussed by D.C. Gordon, *Women of Algeria*, and by Kay Adamson, 'Approaches to the study of women in North Africa', remain a difficult subject. The underlying economic problems have meanwhile generated a substantial literature. Most recently outlined by Bennoune, they are less polemically reviewed by Taher Benhouria, *L'économie de l'Algérie*, and M.E. Benissad, *L'économie algérienne contemporaine*, yet another accompaniment to Ageron in *Que sais-je?* Karen Pfeifer, *Agrarian Reform under State Capitalism*, returns to the fundamental question of agriculture, while Assia Hireche, *Algérie. L'après-pétrole*, assesses the prospects for the future. Nicole Grimaud, *La politique extérieure de l'Algérie (1962–1978)*, evaluates the foreign policy of Algeria under Ben Bella and Boumedienne.

The changes away from the one-party state in the direction of a multi-party political system, which followed the rioting in October 1988, are still in progress, and have not yet produced a formal literature, although cf. e.g. Burgat and Leca, 'La mobilisation islamiste et les élections algériennes de 12 juin 1990'. Nor has the important question of Maghribi unity and its attendant issue, relations between North Africa and the European Common Market. The demise of the East European bloc will surely have its effect upon Algeria, as will the crisis in the Gulf. The relevant volumes of the *Annuaire de l'Afrique du Nord* will eventually provide detailed coverage; meanwhile English-language readers should consult the *Quarterly Economic Review of Algeria* by the Economist Intelligence Unit (EIU), which gives a regular overview of developments and prospects.

WORKS

BY CHARLES-ROBERT AGERON

Histoire de l'Algérie contemporaine, 1st edn, Paris, 1964; 9th edn, *1830–1988*, 1990.
Les Algériens musulmans et la France (1871–1919), 2 vols, Paris, 1968.
Gambetta et la reprise de l'expansion coloniale, Paris, 1972.
Politiques coloniales au Maghreb, Paris, 1973.
L'anticolonialisme en France de 1871 à 1914, Paris, 1973.
France coloniale ou parti colonial?, Paris, 1978.
Histoire de l'Algérie contemporaine, Vol. II, *De l'insurrection de 1871 au déclenchement de la guerre de libération (1954)*, Paris, 1979.
Histoire de la France coloniale, II, *La décolonisation*, Paris, 1990.
'L'Algérie algérienne' de Napoleon III à de Gaulle, Paris, 1980.
Histoire de la France coloniale, Vol. II, *La décolonisation*, Paris, 1990.
'Une politique algérienne libérale sous la IIIe République (1912–1919)', *Revue d'Histoire moderne et contemporaine (RHMC)* (April 1959), 121–51.
'La France a-t-elle eu une politique kabyle?', *Revue historique* (April 1960), 311–52.
'Le mouvement "jeune algérien" ', *Etudes maghrébines. Mélanges offerts à Ch.-A. Julien*, Paris, 1964, 217–43.
'Administration directe ou protectorat: un conflit de méthodes sur l'organisation de la province de Constantine (1837– 1838)', *Revue Française d'Histoire d'Outre-mer (RFHOM)* (May 1964), 5–40.
'Premières négotiations franco-algériennes (le traité Desmichels et le traité de la Tafna)', *Preuves* (Sept. 1964), 44–50; (October 1964), 32–48.

'L'émigration des Musulmans algériens et l'exode de Tlemcen', *Annales ESC*, V (1967), 1047–66.
'La politique kabyle sous le Second Empire', *RFHOM* (Sept. 1967), 67–105.
' 'Abd el-Kader souverain d'un royaume arabe d'Orient', *Revue de l'Occident Musulman et de la Méditerranée (ROMM)*, *Actes du IIe Congrès international d'études nord-africaines* (1970).
'Le premier vote de l'Algérie musulmane. Les élections du collège musulman algérien en 1919–1920', *Revue d'Histoire et de Civilisation du Maghreb* (RIICM) (Jan. 1970), 97–109.
'*Les Algériens musulmans et la France (1971–1919)*', *Revue historique* (April–June 1970), 355–65.
'Fiscalité française et contribuables musulmans dans le Constantinois', *RHCM* (July 1970), 79–94.
'Agriculture socialiste et autogestion rurale en Algerie', *Comptes-rendus trimestriels des séances de l'Académie des Sciences d'Outre-Mer*, XXI, 3 (Nov. 1971), 499–515.
'Ferhat Abbas et l'évolution politique de l'Algérie musulmane pendant la deuxième guerre mondiale', *Revue d'Histoire Maghrebine (RHM)* (July 1975), 125–44.
'L'opinion française devant la guerre d'Algerie', *RFHOM* (May 1976), 256–85.
'Abd el-Kader et la première résistance algérienne', *Les Africains*, ed. Ch.-A. Julien *et al.*, Paris, 1977–8, Vol. I.
'Si M'hammed ben Rahal', *Les Africains*, Vol. VII.
'Les populations du Maghreb face à la propagande allemande pendant la deuxième guerre mondiale', *Revue d'Histoire de la 2e Guerre Mondiale*, no. 114 (1979), 1–39.
'Sur l'année politique 1936', *RHM* (July 1979), 1–33.
'Regards sur la presse politique musulmane dans l'Algérie française', *Cahiers de l'Institut d'Histoire de la Presse et de l'Opinion (CIHPO)*, 5 (1979), 38–88.
'Communisme et nationalisme dans l'Algérie française', *CIHPO*, 5 (1979), 215–88.
'La pétition de l'émir Khaled au President Wilson (mai 1919)', *RHM*, 19–20 (July 1980), 199–206.
'Les classes moyennes dans l'Algérie coloniale: origines, formation et évaluation quantitative', *Les classes moyennes au Maghreb*, Paris, 1980, 52–75.
'Emigration et politique: l'Etoile nord-africaine et le Parti du peuple algerien', *Cahiers de la Mediterranée: Approches des mutations sociales et de la politisation au Maghreb*, Nice, 1981, 7–32.
'Les Juifs d'Algérie de l'abrogation du décret Crémieux à son rétablissement (7 octobre 1940–20 Octobre 1943)', *Yod. Revue des études hébraïques et juives*, 15–16 (Oct. 1982).
'Les troubles du Nord-Constantinois en mai 1945: une tentative insurrectionnelle?', *Vingtième siècle*, 4 (1984).
'L'immigration maghrébine en France', *Vingtième siecle* (July 1985).
'Le gouvernement Mendès-France et l'insurrection algérienne', *Mendès-France et le mendèsisme*, Paris, 1985.
'Le parti communiste algerien', *Vingtième siècle* (Dec. 1986).

Bibliography 155

'Une figure du nationalisme algérien: Ferhat 'Abbas', *Monde Arabe. Maghreb Machrek*, 115 (Jan.–March 1987), 75–9.

'Vers un syndicalisme national en Algérie (1946–1956)', *RHMC* (July–Sept. 1989).

* * *

Abbas, F., *Guerre et révolution d'Algérie*, I, *La nuit coloniale*, Paris, 1962; II, *Autopsie d'une guerre: l'aurore*, Paris, 1980.

Abun-Nasr, J.M. *A History of the Maghrib in the Islamic Period*, Cambridge, 1987.

Académie des Sciences d'Outre-Mer, Hommes et Destins, Paris, 1975–; Vol. VII, *Maghreb Machrek*, 1986.

Adamson, K, 'Approaches to the study of women in North Africa, as reflected in the research of various scholars', *Maghreb Review*, III, 7–8 (1978), 22–31.

Amin, S. *The Maghreb in the Modern World*, Harmondsworth, 1970.

Andrew, C.M., and A.S. Kanya-Forstner, *France Overseas: The Great War and the Climax of French Imperial Expansion*, London, 1981.

Annuaire: see Centre de Recherches (CRESM)

Aron, R., *et al.*, *Les origines de la guerre d'Algérie*, Paris, 1962.

Barbour, N., ed., *A Survey of North West Africa (the Maghrib)*, Oxford, 1959, 1962.

Baroli, M., *La vie quotidienne des français en Algérie, 1830–1914*, Paris, 1967.

Benachenhou, A., *Formation du sous-developpement en Algérie. Essai sur les limites du développement du capitalisme, 1830–1962*, Algiers, 1976.

Benhouria, T., *L'économie de l'Algérie*, Paris, 1980.

Benissad, M.E., *L'économie algérienne contemporaine*, Paris, 1980.

Bennoune, M., *The Making of Contemporary Algeria, 1830–1987*, Cambridge, 1988.

Bernard, A., *L'Algérie*, Paris, 1929.

Berque, J., *Le Maghreb entre deux querres*, 2nd edn, Paris, 1970; Eng. trans., *French North Africa: the Maghreb between Two World Wars*, London, 1967.

Blet, H., *Histoire de la colonisation française*, Paris, 1946.

Bourdieu, P., *The Algerians*, Boston, 1962.

——, *et al. Travail et travailleurs en Algerie*, Paris and the Hague, 1963.

Brett, M., 'Problems in the interpretation of the history of the Maghrib in the light of some recent publications', *J. African History*, XIII (1972), 489–506.

——, 'The colonial period in the Maghrib and its aftermath: the present state of historical writing', *J. African History*, XVII (1976), 291–305.

——, 'Continuity and change: Egypt and North Africa in the nineteenth century', *J. African History*, XXVII (1986), 149–62.

——, 'Les écrits anglais sur la guerre de libération algérien/Writing in English about the Algeria war of liberation', in *Le retentissement de la révolution algérienne*, Colloque internationale d'Alger (24–28 Nov. 1984), Algiers and Brussels, 1985, 235–47.

——, 'The Maghrib', *Cambridge History of Africa*, VII, ch. 6.

——, 'Legislating for inequality in Algeria: the Senatus-Consulte of 14 July 1865', *Bulletin of the School of Oriental and African Studies*, LI (1988), 440–61.

156 Bibliography

British Admiralty (Naval Intelligence Division), *Algeria*, 2 vols, London, 1942-4.

Brunschwig, H., *French Colonialism, 1871-1914: Myths and Realities*, London, 1966.

Burgat, F., with J. Leca, 'La mobilisation islamiste et les élections algériennes du 12 juin 1990', *Monde Arabe: Maghreb Machrek*, 129 (July-Aug.-Sept. 1990), 5-22.

Cambridge History of Africa, The, general editors, J.D. Fage and Roland Oliver, 8 vols, Cambridge, 1975-88; Vols. V- VIII.

Centre de Recherches et d'Etudes sur les Sociétés Méditerranéennes, Aix-en-Provence (CRESM); *Annuaire de l'Afrique du Nord*, 1962-.

Charnay, J.-P., *La vie musulmane en Algérie d'après la jurisprudence de la première moitié du XXe siècle*, Paris, 1965.

Christelow, A., *Muslim Law Courts and the French Colonial State in Algeria*, Princeton, 1985.

——, 'Algerian Islam in a time of transition', *Maghreb Review*, VIII, 5-6 (1983), 124-30.

Clarke, J.I., and W.B. Fisher, eds, *Populations of the Middle East and North Africa*, London, 1972.

Clayton, A., 'Cruelty and terror: The case of the May 1945 Setif uprising in Algeria', paper presented to the Workshop 'Constructing Terror: Violence and Decolonisation', Cambridge, 1991.

Clegg, I., *Workers' Self-Management in Algeria*, London, 1971.

Cobban, A., *A History of Modern France*, II, *1799-1871*; III, *1871-1962*, 2nd edn, Harmondsworth, 1965.

Confer, C.V., *France and Algeria: the Problem of Civil and Political Reform, 1870-1920*, New York, 1966.

Cooke, J.J., *New French Imperialism 1880-1910: The Third Republic and Colonial Expansion*, Newton Abbot and Hamden, 1973.

——, 'Eugène Etienne and the emergence of colon dominance in Algeria, 1884-1905', *The Muslim World*, LXV (1975), 39-53.

——, 'The colonial origins of colon and Muslim nationalism in Algeria, 1880-1920', *Indian Political Science Review*, X (1976), 19-36.

Cubertafond, B., *L'Algérie contemporaine*, Paris, 1981.

Danan, Y.M., *La vie politique à Alger de 1940 à 1944*, Paris, 1963.

Danziger, R., *Abd al-Qadir and the Algerians: Resistance to the French and Internal Consolidation*, New York and London, 1977.

Deschamps, H., *Méthodes et doctrines coloniales de la France du XVI siecle à nos jours*, 2 vols., Paris, 1953.

Despois, J., *L'Afrique du Nord*, Paris, 1949, 1958, 1964.

—— and R. Raynal, *Géographie de l'Afrique du Nord-Ouest*, Paris, 1967.

Dougherty, J.J., *The Politics of Wartime Aid. American Economic Assistance to France and French Northwest Africa, 1940-1946*, Westport, Conn., and London, 1978.

Economist Intelligence Unit (EIU), London, *Quarterly Economic Review of Algeria*

Encyclopaedia of Islam, 2nd edn, Leiden and London, 1955, in progress.

Encyclopédie de l'empire français, Encyclopédie coloniale et maritime: Algérie et Sahara, 2 vols, Paris, 1948.

Entelis, J.P., *Algeria: The Revolution Institutionalized*, London, 1986.

Etienne, B., *L'Algérie. Cultures et revolution*, Paris, 1977.

Fanon, F., *A Dying Colonialism*, London, 1970.

Gallissot, R., *L'économie de l'Afrique du Nord*, Paris, 1969.

——, 'Precolonial Algeria', *Economy and Society*, IV (1975), 418–45.

Gordon, D.C., *The Passing of French Algeria*, London, New York and Toronto, 1966.

——, *Women of Algeria: An essay on change*, Cambridge, Mass., 1972.

Grimaud, N., *La politique extérieure de l'Algérie (1962–1978)*, Paris, 1984.

Gsell, S., G. Marcais, G. Yver, *Histoire de l'Algérie*, Paris, 1927.

Guernier, E., *La Berbérie, l'Islam et la France*, 2 vols, Paris, 1950.

Hardy, G., *Histoire sociale de la colonisation française*, Paris, 1953.

Heggoy, A.A., *Historical Dictionary of Algeria*; *African Historical Dictionaries*, no. 28; Metuchen, NJ, and London, 1981.

Hermassi, E., *Leadership and National Development in North Africa*, Berkeley and Los Angeles, 1973.

Hirèche, A., *Algérie: l'après-pétrole. Quelles stratégies pour 1995 et 2010?*, Paris, 1989.

Hommes et Destins: see Académie des Sciences d'Outre-Mer

Horne, A., *A Savage War of Peace: Algeria 1954–1962*, London, 1977, 1987.

Humbaraci, A., *Algeria: A Revolution that Failed. A Political History since 1954*, London, 1966.

Issawi, C., *An Economic History of the Middle East and North Africa*, New York, 1982.

Jackson, H.F., *The FLN in Algeria: party development in a revolutionary society*, Westport, Conn., and London, 1977.

Johnson, D., 'Algeria: some problems of modern history', *J. African History*, V (1964), 221–42.

Julien, Ch.-A., *Histoire de l'Afrique du Nord*, 1st edn, Paris, 1931; 2nd edn, 2 vols, to 1830 only, Paris, 1951–2. Eng. trans. and edn Vol. II, J. Petrie and C. C. Stewart, *History of North Africa: Tunisia, Algeria, Morocco. From the Arab Conquest to 1830*, London, 1970.

——, *L'Afrique du Nord en marche*, 3rd edn, Paris, 1972.

——, *Histoire de l'Algerie contemporaine*, I, *Conquête et colonisation*, Paris, 1964.

——, *Les Africains*, (et al., ed.), 12 vols, Paris, 1977–8.

Kaddache, M., *La vie politique à Alger de 1919 à 1939*, Algiers, 1970.

——, *Histoire du nationalisme algérien*, 2 vols, Algiers, 1980–1.

Kedourie, E., 'The retreat from Algeria', in *idem, Islam in the Modern World*, London, 1980.

Khenouf, M., and M. Brett, 'Algerian nationalism and the Allied military strategy and propaganda during the Second World War: the background to Setif', in D. Killingray and R. Rathbone, eds, *Africa and the Second World War*, London, 1986, 258–74.

Knapp, W., *North West Africa: A Political and Economic Survey*, Oxford, 1977.

Lacheraf, M., *L'Algérie: nation et société*, Paris, 1965.

Lacoste, Y., A. Nouschi, A. Prenant, *L'Algérie passé et présent. Le cadre et les étages de la constitution de l'Algérie actuelle*, Paris, 1960.

158   *Bibliography*

Laroui, A., *The History of the Maghrib*, Princeton, 1977.
Lazreg, M., *The Emergence of Classes in Algeria. A study of colonialism and socio-political change*, Boulder, Colo., 1976.
Lawless, R.I., *Algeria: World Bibliographical Series*, vol. 19; Oxford and Santa Barbara, 1980.
———, *Algerian Bibliography: English Language Publications 1830–1973*, London and New York, 1976.
Le Tourneau, R., *Evolution politique de l'Afrique du Nord musulmane, 1920–1961*, Paris, 1962.
Leca, J., *L'Algérie politique: institutions et régime*, Paris, 1975.
Lee, R.D., 'Regional politics in a unitary system: colonial Algeria, 1920–1954', Ph.D, Columbia, 1972; microfilm reprint, Ann Arbor and London, 1978.
Les Africains, see Ch.-A. Julien *et al.*, eds.
Lucas, P., and J.-C. Vatin, *L'Algérie des anthropologues*, Paris, 1982.
Martin, B.G., 'Opposition to French colonialism in Algeria: 'Abd al-Qadir, his predecessors and rivals', in *idem, Muslim Brotherhoods in Nineteenth-Century Africa*, Cambridge, 1976.
Martin, C., *Histoire de l'Algérie française*, 2 vols, Paris, 1979.
Memmi, A., *The Colonizer and the Colonized*, London, 1974.
Merad, A., *Le réformisme musulman en Algérie de 1925 à 1940*, Paris and The Hague, 1967.
Meynier, G., *L'Algérie révélée. La guerre de 1914–1918 et le premier quart du XXe siècle*, Geneva, 1981.
Morsy, M., *North Africa 1800–1900: A Survey from the Nile to the Atlantic*, London and New York, 1984.
Nouschi, A., *Enquête sur le niveau de vie des populations rurales Constantinoises de la conquête jusqu'en 1919*, Paris, 1961.
———, *La naissance du nationalisme algérien, 1914–1954*, Paris, 1962.
Ottaway, D. and M., *Algeria: the Politics of a Socialist Revolution*, Berkeley and Los Angeles, 1970.
Perkins, K.J., *Qaids, Captains and Colons: French Military Administration in the Colonial Maghrib*, New York, 1981.
Pfeifer, K., *Agrarian Reform under State Capitalism in Algeria*, Westport, Conn., and London, 1985.
Playfair, Sir R. Lambert, 'A Bibliography of Algeria from the Expedition of Charles V in 1541 to 1887'; 'Supplement to the Bibliography of Algeria from the Earliest Times to 1895'; reprinted in *idem, The Bibliography of the Barbary States*, 2 vols, Gregg International Publishers, n.p. , 1971, vol. II.
Porch, D., *The Conquest of the Sahara*, London, 1985.
Powers, D.S., 'Orientalism, colonialism and legal history: The attack on Muslim family endowments in Algeria and India', *Comparative Studies in Society and History*, XXXI (1989), 535–71.
Prochaska, D., *Making Algeria French: Colonialism in Bône, 1870–1920*, Cambridge and Paris, 1990.
Quandt, W.B., *Revolution and Political Leadership: Algeria, 1954–1968*, Cambridge, Mass., 1969.

Rey-Goldzeiguer, A., *Le royaume arabe. La politique algérienne de Napoleon III, 1861–1870*, Algiers, 1977.

Richardson, M.L., 'French Algeria between the wars: nationalism and colonial reform, 1919–1939', Ph.D, Duke University, 1975; microfilm reprint, Ann Arbor and London, 1978.

Roberts, H., 'The Kabyle question in contemporary Algeria', *Government and Opposition*, XVII, 3 (1982).

Roberts, S., *History of French Colonial Policy, 1870–1925*, London, 1927.

Ruedy, J., *Land Policy in Colonial Algeria: The Origins of the Rural Public Domain*, Berkeley and Los Angeles, 1967.

Service Historique de l'Armée de la Terre, *La guerre d'Algérie par les documents*, I, *L'avertissement 1943–1946*, Paris, 1990.

Sivan, E., *Communisme et nationalisme en Algérie*, Paris, 1976.

Spencer, W., *Algiers in the Age of the Corsairs*, Norman, Oklahoma, 1976.

Stora, B., *Dictionnaire biographique de militants nationalistes algériens 1926–54: E.N.A, P.P.A.-M.T.L.D.*, Paris, 1985.

——, *Messali Hadj*, Paris, 1982.

Sullivan, A.T., *Thomas-Robert Bugeaud. France and Algeria, 1784–1849: Politics, power and the good society*, Hamden, Connecticut, 1983.

Taleb, A., Ibrahimi, *De la décolonisation à la révolution culturelle (1962–1972)*, Algiers, 1981.

Temimi, A., *Le Beylik de Constantine et Hadj Ahmed Bey (1830–1837)*, Tunis, 1978.

——, ed., *Revue d'Histoire Maghrébine*, 1972–.

Tiano, A., *Le Maghreb entre les mythes*, Paris, 1967..

——, *Le développement économique du Maghreb*, Paris, 1968.

Tlemcani, R., *State and Revolution in Algeria*, Boulder, Colo., and London, 1986.

UNESCO General History of Africa, 8 vols, Paris, London and Berkeley, 1981–; vols VI–VIII.

Valensi, L., *On the Eve of Colonialism: North Africa before the French Conquest, 1790–1830*, New York and London, 1977.

Vatin, J.C., *L'Algérie politique. Histoire et société*, Paris, 1974.

——, 'Religious resistance and state power in Algeria', in A.S. Cudsi and A.E.H. Dessouki, eds, *Islam and Power*, London, 1981, ch. 8.

——, 'Popular puritanism versus state reformism: Islam in Algeria', in J.P. Piscatori, ed., *Islam in the Political Process*, Cambridge, 1983.

Von Sivers, P., 'Alms and arms: The combative saintliness of the Awlad Sidi Shaykh in the Algerian Sahara, sixteenth-nineteenth centuries', *Maghreb Review*, VIII, 5–6 (1983), 113–23.

——, 'Insurrection and accommodation: Indigenous leadership in eastern Algeria, 1840–1900', *Int. J. Middle Eastern Studies*, VI (1975), 259–75.

——, 'Algerian landownership and rural leadership, 1860–1914: A quantitative approach', *Maghreb Review*, IV, 2 (1979), 58–62.

——, 'Indigenous administrators in Algeria, 1846–1914: Manipulation and manipulators', *Maghreb Review*, VII, 5–6 (1982), 116–21.

Wansbrough, J., 'The decolonization of North African history', *J. African History*, IX (1968), 643–50.

Zagoria, J.D., 'The rise and fall of the movement of Messali Hadj in Algeria, 1924–1954', Ph.D, Columbia, 1973; microfilm reprint, Ann Arbor and London, 1978.

Zartmann, I.W., *Government and Politics in Northern Africa*, London, 1964, ch. 3, 'Algeria'.

INDEX

Abd el-Kader, 11, 12, 12n, 13, 14, 15, 17, 18, 19, 20, 22, 23, 51, 79
'achour (Qur'anic tithes), 17, 23
Africa Battalions, 2
Africa Concessions, 6
Agéron, Charles-Robert, vi, vii
agha (commander), 11, 17, 22, 23, 34
Ahmad of Constantine, 15
Ait Ahmed, 106, 114, 137
Algeria, Algerian (Colonial): abortive revolution (1898–1900), 63–4; administration, 14–28, 29, 35, 36, 37, 73, 75, 102; agriculture, 22, 25, 30, 31, 32, 33, 37n, 43, 60, 66, 85, 87, 88, 99, 113, 119; (arable), 32, 33, 44, 60, 61, 66, 67, 84, 85, 86, 87, 90; (pastoral), 26, 29–30, 31, 33, 66, 67, 68, 86, 87, 88; Assembly, 104, 105, 106, 111, 113; assimilation, 24, 26–7, 28, 34, 35, 39, 45, 53–7, 70, 71, 74, 77, 83, 95, 96, 98, 103, 111, 120; association, 37, 40, 41, 74, 120; business, 85; citizenship, 62, 93; civil territory, 22, 24, 29, 45, 54–5, 65; colonisation, 22, 24–7, 30, 31, 32, 37, 43, 45–6, 47, 52–3, 57–64, 82, 83; crime, 67; economy, 21, 31, 32, 33, 38, 44, 62, 64, 75, 82–92, 99, 101, 102; education, 21, 28, 34, 39, 42–3, 95; elections; 102–3; electoral colleges, 104–5, 118–19; French conquest of, 9–27 passim; industry, 38, 89, 90, 99; infrastructure, 44, 80, 91; insurrection (1871), 49–50, 51, 52–3; land policy, 25–6, 29, 31, 32, 36, 38–9, 45–6, 52, 57–63, 69, 99; local government, 3, 28, 29; members of Parliament, 56; military regime, 37–44; military territory, 22, 23, 29, 45, 54–5; Ministry of, 34–7; Morocco and,

19; naturalisation, 39, 62–3; political reform 78, 93–107; poverty, 68, 90; press, 50, 80, 94; property rights, 29; restricted occupation (1837–40), 14–18; sequestration, 52–3, 56; Service de l'Algérie, 56; settler supremacy, 45, 53, 47–64 (see also colons); total conquest, 18–22; trade unions, 113; unemployment, 88; urbanisation, 62, 69, 82, 88; War, 108–28 passim
Algeria, Algerian (Independent): agrarian reform, 132, 133, 134, 140; agriculture, 134, 140, 142; 'Algerianisation', 132, 135–6, 139 (see also Arabisation); Algerian Revolution, 132; civil war, 129; demography, 134, 141, 142–3; economy, 138; education, 135, 136, 139, 141, emigration, 134, 135, 140; and EC, 135, 137; foreign aid, 135, 138; foreign policy, 136–7; Four-Year Plan, 138, 139, 142; Franco-Algerian relations, 134; free elections, 142–4; industry, 138, 139, 140, 141, 142; Islamic fundamentalism, 143–4; land reform, 133; National Charter, 138; nationalisation, 133, 138, 140; oil and gas, 134, 135, 138, 139, 142; one-party state, 132; referendum, 132; trade, 133, 140; unemployment, 134, 140, 142
Algiers: 3, 5, 7, 9, 11, 13, 14, 23, 29, 36, 40, 42, 47, 64, 85, 98, 112, 115, 122, 125, 129, 131, 138, 143; 'Battle of', 115; capture of, 6; commune of (1870–1), 48–9; Napoleon III visits, 36, 38
anti-clericalism, 35, 51, 71
anti-Semitism, 63, 64, 83, 98
Arabs: 5, 7, 29; Arabisation, 2, 73, 105, 135, 136, 141; Arabism, 93;

161